This book is dedicated to:

Mary Jo—for your love, encouragement and support, even if you thought this adventure was sort of crazy;

and to...

Drew and Sam—may you find many adventures of your own.

Pedaling the Pioneer Path

*A Journey Down
Michigan's Territorial Road*

*To Michael —
Enjoy the journey!
Chuck Jager*

Chuck Jager

Illustrations by Janet Frazier

As I knelt by the side of the road, the heavens poured down on my head. But I looked westward, toward a clearing sky.

My head bowed low and the rain seeped through my helmet's vents as I examined my flat tire.

One hundred eighty two years earlier, Eleazar Morton passed this very spot. This was Michigan's Territorial Road, a historic trail that brought countless pioneers westward across the state to new frontier homesteads.

Perhaps Eleazar had trouble here also—a broken axle, or a covered wagon stuck in the mud. Maybe he was, like me, wet and discouraged.

Eleazar's purpose was to forge a new life for his family in southwest Michigan. As for me, the adventure of this five day solo bicycle trip was overshadowed by questions about the rest of my life. Although generations apart, Eleazar Morton and I both trekked the Territorial Road seeking a fresh start.

Eleazar may have very well fixed his broken wagon wheel and extricated his mud-stuck wagon with his own two hands, but like many pioneers, strangers may have helped him as well. Perhaps a fellow traveler may have stopped, or Eleazar may have walked back to a frontier cabin the family had passed.

For me, I remembered a friendly resident back down the road. A bit earlier, we had passed some time together, sharing news of the road.

My hero was Dave, who lived in a ranch-style house up the road. Now, with me in distress at his doorstep, Dave had the pioneer mentality of helping travelers along the road. I pulled my bicycle into his garage. With his tools and know-how, he had me back traveling the wilderness path soon enough.

I hope the Mortons had similar help.

It might seem strange that I was riding a bicycle across Michigan, following a road built in the 1830's. It certainly was peculiar, odd, and worrisome to my wife and mother. They are normal people. I, however, am a slightly-introverted bicycle-riding history teacher in the midst of a mid-life crisis, who once lived on Territorial Road and volunteers for a museum started by a pioneer who traveled this road. For me, then, this wasn't an odd adventure at all. It felt more like destiny.

The idea for taking this trip came to me as I sat on the front porch of the Morton House Museum, the oldest house in Benton Harbor, in the southwestern corner of the state ("Michigan's Great Southwest," as the local boosters call it.) The Mortons built this house in 1849, and gussied it up with classical pillars and birdseye maple trim in 1912.

I served on the board of this museum because it was a way to do history, and it seemed a means to make my little corner of the world a better place. The museum is a wonderful Benton Harbor institution, where a group of ladies hold the place together with stories, memories, and desserts. My job is to stay out of the kitchen and try to make myself useful by setting up chairs and brainstorming compelling historical happenings.

As I sat on an old wicker chair on the Morton House porch, the spring sun shining over my shoulder, I had an itch to go on an adventure. Eleazar Morton's adventure was to cross the wilderness of Michigan to this house. My adventure would be to follow his route on my bicycle.

I wanted this, though, to be more than an adventure. This journey could be a new start for me, just as it was for Eleazar. This would be a journey from the settled world of being a teacher, to the wilderness of writing.

Like many others, I had long hoped to be a writer. The main obstacle in my way was that I didn't write. Writers write, and I didn't. Here was a chance to set out in the writer's version of a covered wagon, hoping at some point to reach the new home of a writer's life.

The bicycle trip along the Territorial Road would give me the reason to write, give me a goal to write, and kick me in the butt to write. I would write what I love to read—narrative nonfiction, telling the story of the author's role in an adventurous trip. I'd always wanted to write a book. This was my idea, my chance.

Sitting on the Morton porch, dreaming of the writer's life, I could look out the window at a large boulder next to the Territorial Road. I knew that boulder marked the end of the road, but where did it begin? How did that road meander across Michigan? Could I find traces of that old road today?

Gradually, a plan formed in my mind. I decided to follow the Territorial Road. I would trace, as closely as possible, the original route of Michigan pioneers: from Detroit to Benton Harbor, from Motown to the Morton House. Not only that, but I would be following the path of the Mortons, the founding family of Benton Harbor and the builders of the historic home in which I sat.

A wagon pulled by oxen seemed too authentic. (Plus, I wasn't really clear on the difference between an ox and a cow.) Instead, I would ride my bike, pulling a Burley trailer that I could call a wagon. I would be the ox.

The old Territorial Road stretched for about 200 miles across the lower palm of the mitten of the Lower Peninsula of Michigan. I might travel a bit faster than the original pioneers, but planned more stops to explore the road and the history alongside it. Thus, I found myself on a sunny June morning in Detroit, about to pedal off on the Territorial Road.

Day One
Tuesday, June 23, 2015
Detroit to Ann Arbor

The Pioneer Morton Family—Setting off through Downtown Detroit—
Bicycling Background—A John Waters Homage—Through Corktown
with a Visit to Tiger Stadium—Father Gabriel Richard—Outfitted for a
Journey—The Dictator of Dearborn—Ten Eyck, the Dutchman—
Dearborn History—Annie's Ghost—Denise and Rudy—Why a Bike?—
Washtenaw to Ann Arbor

I was standing in the middle of Campus Martius, the lively, busy central plaza of downtown Detroit. Here, like the spokes of a bicycle wheel, the various central thoroughfares branch out toward the rest of Michigan. I was headed down Michigan Avenue, but I actually had a choice of six roads that met here at Campus Martius. This somewhat nutty street plan was the brainchild of Augustus Woodward, who laid out the original downtown streets in 1805. Thomas L. McKenney wrote a book in 1827, in which he commented on Woodward's plan:

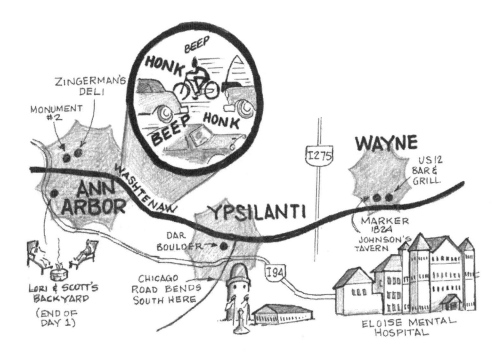

ZINGERMAN'S
DELI

MONUMENT
#2

BEEP

HONK

HONK

BEEP

WAYNE

I275

US 12
BAR &
GRILL

ANN
ARBOR

WASHTENAW

YPSILANTI

MARKER
182A
JOHNSON'S
TAVERN

LORI & SCOTT'S
BACKYARD

(END OF
DAY 1)

DAR
BOULDER

CHICAGO
ROAD BENDS
SOUTH HERE

I 94

ELOISE MENTAL
HOSPITAL

8

"I have seen a plot of this city. I wish for the sake of its designer, towards whom, personally, I entertain the kindest feelings, that it have never been conceived by him. It looks pretty on paper, but is fanciful; and resembles one of those octagonal spider webs which you have seen in a dewy morning, with a centre, you know, and lines leading out to points around the circumference, and fastened to spires of grass. The citizens of Detroit would do well, in my opinion, and their posterity would thank them for it, were they to reduce the network of that plan to something practical and regular."

Or as another author put it in 1838, it was "better suited...to flatter the fancy than to promote practical utility."

As I sat at a table under the trees and soldiers' monuments, I envisioned myself in the shoes of those early Michigan pioneers. One of these travelers was Eleazar Morton, whose house awaited me at the other end of the Territorial Road. Eleazar, like most migrants to Michigan, arrived in Detroit, likely via a boat trip through Lake Erie. Back in the day, this was about a 40 hour trip on the lake. Before boarding for the lake trip, most of the migrants would have traveled on the new Erie Canal, completed in 1825 and stretching across the state of New York.

Eleazar had moved with his family to New York when he was about 20. From Massachusetts, they descended from an early Pilgrim, George Morton, who arrived in 1623, just two ships after the Mayflower. Another ancestor fought against the Indians in King Phillip's War in 1675, and Eleazar's father fought against the British in the Revolutionary War.

When Eleazar arrived in Detroit in 1834, he and his family might have filled the boat. Eleazar and his wife Joanna had 10 kids, ranging from age 23 down to eight years old. Perhaps the Mortons had a convoy of wagons here in Detroit waiting to travel down the Territorial Road to Benton Harbor. It seems unlikely that they and all their stuff would fit into one wagon.

The Morton family was part of what was called "Michigan Fever," as emigrants from the east poured into the territory. According to one 20th century historian, the Michigan Territory grew faster than any other place in America in the decade of the 1830's.

The Mortons and I were both following the same route, but our experiences would be very different. While Detroit was new to Eleazar and his family, it was still a familiar setting for them. This stretch across the wilderness of Michigan was a journey into the unknown. For me, the reverse was true. Detroit was unknown territory, and the more I rode toward home, the more familiar the surroundings would become.

On a beautiful, breezy day, I set out to follow the path of Eleazar Morton and other pioneers of the 1830's. Young hipsters filled the streets, walking to their jobs at Compaq and J.P. Morgan. Detroit may be a ghost town in many places, but here it was bustling. I only saw a few bicycles, but a Zagster bicycle rental station was off to the side.

Plenty of energy before setting off from downtown Detroit

I had taken a few minutes earlier to ride a couple of blocks to the waterfront of the Detroit River. It is a tradition of cyclists to do the "wheel dip" to give us a sense of full completion of a trip. Cross-country cyclists dip their rear wheels in one ocean and then the front wheels in the other ocean at the end of their journeys. Cyclists on RAGBRAI (The Register's Annual Great Bicycle Ride Across Iowa) start with their rear wheels in the Missouri River, and finish with dipping the front wheels in the Mississippi River. I wanted to have a similar ceremonial sense of completion on this cross-state ride.

This proved a difficult tradition to fulfill. I rode my bike through Hart Plaza near the Renaissance Center. I would have to enter a restricted area and jump a security chain just to get to the river. I sat on a bench for a few minutes to ponder whether I should do this. All my life I've been the good kid, the rule-follower, the non-rebellious son. This day I proposed to live life a bit more fully and bravely. *Carpe diem*. I breached the "No Entry" signs and climbed over the chains. Of course, there was no gradual riverbank or beach to walk down to the water. I had to lift my bike over a rail, lean over, and dangle the back tire into the water. I imagined my trip ending before it began if my hands slipped and I dropped my bicycle to the river bottom. I also wondered if, in a similar spot late some night in the past, some mobsters had held Jimmy Hoffa over a similar railing. Thankfully, nothing dropped into the river this day. My back bicycle tire was now wet from the waters of the eastern edge of Michigan. The "wheel dip" tradition would be fulfilled when I dipped my front wheel in Lake Michigan after crossing the state. This baptism of the bike in the Detroit River signified the start of my journey down the Territorial Road and down the next stage of my life.

I was apprehensive about many things on this trip, but I knew in my heart that a bicycle was the way to travel. For most people, riding a bike is a cherished memory of childhood. I've forgotten much from when I was a kid, but I can still clearly see that day when my dad started pushing me down our suburban street, and then realizing he was no longer pushing: I was riding a bike! I can see also the spot at the end of the street where I crashed the bike in an open field. I now knew how to ride, but I still didn't know how to stop or turn around.

Unlike many other adults, though, I am still a little kid when it comes to riding a bike. Bicycling makes me feel like I am eight years old again (maybe nine, when I knew how to stop and turn around). I love to ride the bike trails with my kids while camping, and a Saturday morning bike ride is a wonderful way to start a weekend.

Mostly, though, I am a bike commuter. I often ride my bike to school. As I carry my bike up the stairs, I get many strange looks from the teenage students. I try to get them to remember what fun riding a bicycle was for them, many years ago before they became too cool.

I've had little luck getting students to participate, but I always try to ride my bike on "Ride Your Bike to Work Day" in May. It's an easy three miles or so for me currently, but I did it as an 11 mile ride when I was commuting from Benton Harbor to Lakeshore High School, and rode about 30 miles one year from Benton Harbor to Niles Brandywine High School. I had to leave for work at 4 a.m. that day.

This trip would also be a great opportunity to see what the bicycling environment was like across the state, and perhaps generate enthusiasm and awareness of riding bicycles. I love the notion of Michigan and America being bike-centric instead of focused on cars. I love to see people getting in shape on bicycles, saving gas, and helping the environment. There seems to be a definite bicycle movement afoot across the land, and I not only wanted to talk to people about the history of Michigan and the Territorial Road, but also explore the current bicycle scene. (And also enjoy the irony of desiring a bike-centric society while standing in the middle of "Motown.")

Back at Campus Martius, I pointed my bike west, into the wind, ready to start my grand adventure. I discovered at the next intersection that it was not west, and this was not the Territorial Road. It was Fort Street, going southwest. Not one block into my trip, I was going the wrong way!

This initial misstep reminded me of the night before, lying in bed unable to sleep. My wife had driven me to Detroit, where she would kiss me goodbye and I would ride back home to her. As I lay in bed in the hotel room, hour after unsleeping hour, I channeled John Waters' road trip book, *Carsick*. Waters gives three versions of his cross-country automobile trip. In the first imaginary trip, everything goes as well as it can. In the second part of the book, he conjures up every horrific possibility. Finally, he tells the true story of the trip.

In the spirit of John Waters, I laid there imagining the perfect trip and the nightmare trip. In my perfect trip, I have great weather with a steady wind at my back the whole time. My new lime green bike feels fast and comfortable. I meet interesting characters along the way and make life-long friendships. I have adventures—some problems to overcome, some danger, some thrilling and uplifting moments. People along the way show me some amazing sights. I'm able to camp in some unusual, but safe spots. I find some spots where the Territorial Road is hidden to most folks, but I'm able to follow it, giving me some sense of how it was in the 1830's. I get some great press coverage—newspapers,

TV news, Michigan's Big Show, with radio host Michael Patrick Shiels. As I near the end of the trip in Benton Harbor, dozens of people turn out to cheer my arrival.

Or...

The nightmare trip starts in Detroit with me getting harassed and mugged. At some point my bike gets stolen and I have to rent a replacement (a pink girl's bike with a slow leak in the back tire) to finish the trip. I'm too unfriendly or scared or oblivious to talk to anyone along the way. The weather alternates between muggy heat and rain, and my tent leaks. A steady wind is directly in my face, except when it turns gusty. I have to pedal far out of my way to camp at an RV park with no trees, no space, and no privacy, and no one comes out of their RV to interact with me. I miss appointments to visit sites. I get lost several times. There is no adventure. Nothing interesting happens on the trip. It is just monotonous pedaling, interrupted by insignificant local historical sites that no one cares about. My bike breaks down, and my mother has to pick me up and drive me home 40 miles short of the end.

I mentally put disaster out of my mind, came back to reality and restarted my trip. I backtracked a block to Campus Martius. I found the road headed west toward Lake Michigan. I reset my bike computer to zeros, and then started my journey down the old Territorial Road. In a sense, I was resetting my life, and starting my life journey down a new road.

Here the old road was now Michigan Avenue, an apt name for a road that stretches across the state. Only a block or two later I spotted the first sign of the past. Attached to the side of the Holiday Inn Express on the corner of Michigan Avenue and Washington Street, a Michigan state historical marker described the Territorial Road. One of the luxuries of this solo trip was the ability to stop at every historical marker, without the groans and eye-rolling of my two teen-aged sons. A bit further down is the exuberant and victorious General Kosciuszko statue. He was a Polish general who, inspired by Thomas Jefferson's words in the Declaration of Independence, came to America (starting his own new journey) and played an important role in defeating the British in the Revolutionary War.

A few more blocks down Michigan Avenue brought me to Corktown, originally an Irish neighborhood named by the early immigrants who came from County Cork. This area boomed with immigrants in the early days of Detroit, prospered in the glory days of the early 20th century, declined after the 1967 riots, and now is part of Motown's resurgence. It is part of hip

Detroit, a foodie oasis with interesting places to drink and shop. Among those shops is my favorite, John K. King Used and Rare Books. Imagine a million books on four floors piled into a warehouse heaven.

At the corner of Michigan and Trumbull is a site sacred to many Detroiters and Michiganders—old Tiger Stadium. This is where Ty Cobb, Hank Greenberg, and Al Kaline thrilled the local fans. Although the stadium was torn down in stages between 2008 and 2009, the field remained, with home plate, the pitching mound, and the bases. The gate was partly open, so I got off my bike and went in. I stood at home plate and tried to imagine the stadium as it once was. A forlorn baseball lay near the mound.

A local Corktown resident, John, came into the field with his German Shepherd. We talked as his dog squatted just beyond where All-Star shortstop Alan Trammell once patrolled. John was a sign of hope in Detroit. He was "from the burbs," and now lived in Corktown. While the population of Detroit overall has plummeted, the number of white residents like John has increased.

Tiger Stadium is gone, but a field of dreams remains

A few blocks west on Michigan Avenue, the empty shell of the magnificent Michigan Central Railroad station stood off to my left. I almost kept going, but couldn't resist going back to leer at what has been termed "ruin porn." Websites and foreign tourists are apparently fascinated by the many abandoned old buildings in Detroit. The Michigan Central station is the most prominent of these. The structure seems to have narrowly avoided demolition, and currently new, but historically incorrect, windows were going in.

The station is also a reminder that the railroad made the Territorial Road a short-lived travel choice for immigrants to Michigan. The Michigan Central tracks crossed the state in 1850, less than 20 years after the Territorial Road was built. The railroad followed approximately the same route, ducking southwest at Kalamazoo to head to New Buffalo and Chicago instead of St. Joseph and Benton Harbor. The railroad became the main mode of transportation across the state—at least until the advent of the automobile.

West of the station, Michigan Avenue became block after block of run-down and abandoned buildings. Concerned about traffic and the sketchy nature of the neighborhoods on the west side of Detroit, I (and especially my wife) was worried about riding a bike down this stretch of Michigan Avenue. Neither was a problem. If crime is a problem here, it's unlikely to be one at 8:30 a.m. The traffic was surprisingly light with I-94 paralleling this stretch. And I did have a bike lane for part of the way.

Not far from Michigan Avenue in this part of Detroit is St. Anne's Church. The 19th century pastor of this church, Gabriel Richard, was the first Catholic priest in Congress. He apparently liked to wear his brass-rimmed glasses on his forehead, making him a literal "four-eyes" in his portraits.

Father Richard was my kind of Catholic. I was not a "cradle Catholic" like my wife. I joined the Catholic

Church after we got married, mainly to have a common faith for my family, but I was also very attracted by the social justice movement in the church. Gabriel Richard did not just distribute communion wafers and hear confessions; he acted on his faith to make the world a better place. He brought the first printing press to Michigan and printed the first newspaper. He started a number of schools, including those for girls and Native Americans, and was part of the effort to start the University of Michigan in 1817.

Most importantly for my trip, while he was in Congress (as a non-voting delegate, since Michigan was not yet a state) he secured funding for the Chicago Road between Detroit and Fort Dearborn. He was also the originator of the motto of Detroit, *Speramus meliora; resurget cineribus* or, *We hope for better things; it will arise from the ashes.* Coined by Father Richard as he helped rebuild the city from the devastating fire of 1805, their motto perhaps endures as most relevant today. The nadir of the city of Detroit was the downward dip between the fiery riots of 1967 and the Devil's Night torchings in the 1980's. Detroit today is hoping for, and achieving, better things.

Ironically for Motown, a city built by and for the automobile, its current renaissance can mostly clearly be seen in its bike scene. The city has added a multitude of bicycle lanes, including the unique DeQuindre Cut, an old railroad that cuts through the center of the city. Detroit has spawned a new industry in hand-crafted bicycles. Shinola sells high-end bicycles with last-century names (assembled in Detroit) next to high-end watches and leather goods. Detroit Bikes aims to lead a resurgence of American-made bikes. And then there are the group bike rides—like Slow Roll Detroit, part community ride and inner-city party night. Bicycle lovers can Bike the Bridge (the Ambassador Bridge to Canada), or ride in the yearly Tour De Troit. Cyclists and their bikes are helping Detroit rise from the ashes.

About six miles and 45 minutes out from Campus Martius, I crossed over Interstate 94, the modern-day successor to Territorial Road. This was the first of what would be many encounters with I-94 on this trip. Just as the Territorial Road replaced the old Indian trails, and the paved roads replaced the Territorial Road, I-94 became the most recent trail between Detroit and Lake Michigan. Here, at the border between Dearborn and Detroit, the interstate bent south on its way to Metro Detroit airport. It would be another 35 miles before I met up again with I-94, with another eight crossings before the end of the trip.

I felt well-prepared for my adventure along the Territorial Road. My bicycle was a neon-green Trek, a recent gift from my worried mother. It rolled well down the road compared to the 25-year-old clunker that it replaced. It was outfitted with a bike computer, which enabled me to keep track of miles to the next planned stop, and to motivate me to keep my speed up when it lagged. I had a pair of well-padded bike shorts, but baggy—not skin-tight. With two teenage sons and an army of students out there that might see me in public, I did not feel comfortable breaching the Spandex barrier into the serious biking nation. I also had not yet adopted the bike shoes that snap into the pedals. My normal shorts and shoes, though, on this trip allowed me to easily hop off my bike to visit museums and eat at restaurants without a change in attire.

I stowed my gear in a Burley trailer, bought originally to pull my toddler boys who are now eye-rolling teenagers. The Burley liked low places. It pushed me as I went down a hill, but as I tried to ride up the other side of a valley, the Burley wanted to keep me from climbing.

The trailer had an orange flag that provided crucial visibility to motorists. It also served as a weather indicator. I could check wind direction, and when it was wet, I knew it was raining.

The Burley, in some strange and distant way, was also a connection to the people whose path I was tracing. My trailer was a modern version of the covered wagons pulled by the pioneers' oxen. An eponymous "chuck" wagon, if you will.

Me and the Burley, with a happy orange flag

William Least Heat Moon, in his famous travel book *Blue Highways,* compared the prairie schooners used by traveling pioneers to the sails of ships being pushed by the wind across the vast plains. I wasn't sure I liked this analogy for my trip. I knew that the wind would not push my Burley, and one of my most persistent worries was a strong headwind.

The Burley held a small tent, a sleeping bag and pad, snacks, a writing pad and pen, and a small bag of extra clothes. I also had a pioneer-like flip phone. The weight of Burley probably slowed me by a couple of miles an hour, but it also made me a more prominent presence on the road, with fewer near misses by cars. I also carried a water-proof rain jacket, which, along with some new water-proof shoes, made riding in the rain almost pleasant. Famed explorer Sir Ranulph Fiennes once said, "There's no bad weather, only inappropriate clothing."

For added safety, my bike featured a rear-view mirror, a handy addition on crowded four-lane roads. I also made a sign for the back of the Burley that said, "Riding the Territorial Road: From Motown to the Morton House." I also had signs on the trailer thanking sponsors, including Mom.

The six lanes of Interstate 94, plus the median and exit and entrance ramps, provided an effective buffer between the grime and crime of Detroit and the sanitized suburb of Dearborn. Just to make sure, a half-mile stretch of open green space separates the two cities. While many times on this trip only a sign indicated a new city or jurisdiction, one cannot miss the border between Detroit and Dearborn.

A short bike ride into Dearborn brought me past a statue of the gentleman who made sure that Dearborn stayed sanitized, Mayor Orville Hubbard. Hubbard reminds us that racial segregation was not only a southern thing. Known as the "Dictator of Dearborn," Hubbard served 15 consecutive terms, ruling the city from 1942 to 1978. His campaign slogan was "Keep Dearborn Clean," which was widely interpreted to mean keeping out blacks coming from neighboring Detroit. Only 20 African-Americans resided in Dearborn when Hubbard stopped being mayor in 1978. Dearborn's total population that year was 90,000. And he was in denial about it. Sort of.

"I'm not racist," Hubbard once commented, "but I just hate those black bastards."

The Michigan Historical Marker near his statue also got white-washed. It has nothing but positive things to say about Hubbard (it also misspells paid as "payed"). James Loewen's book, *Lies Across America: What American Historic Sites Get Wrong,* discusses the misleading history on the Honorable Mayor Hubbard.

As I would see later in my trip, Michigan has had many proud moments in social justice for the underdog. Mayor Hubbard, however, was an embarrassment to our state. It was with some satisfaction, then, that Mayor Hubbard recently got the boot from his pedestal on Michigan Avenue. Perhaps partly because of the recent controversy over the Confederate flag, Dearborn decided to move Hubbard's statue to the backyard of the local historical society.

With the "Dictator of Dearborn"

Should they have just melted it down? I don't think so. History shouldn't be just wiped out, no matter how repellent it is to us today. Relocating this racist icon to a less prominent location, with some truth-telling historical interpretation, seems like the right solution. As the Civil War was winding down, Abraham Lincoln took a walking tour of Richmond, the conquered Confederate capital. He walked past Libby Prison, the notorious lockup for Northern soldiers. Recently-freed blacks walking with the President volunteered to pull down the prison. "No," Lincoln said. "Leave it as a monument."

One wonders what Hubbard would make of Dearborn today. He died in 1982, just before Dearborn became home to one of the country's largest populations of Arab-Americans. Along the route of the Territorial Road is the Arab American National Museum, which opened in 2005.

Just across the Southfield Freeway, which divides the eastern and western parts of Dearborn, I hopped off my bike to check out the historical marker at the site of the former Ten Eyck Tavern. Although I had been on the road for only about an hour, this would have been a full day's journey for the Morton family and other pioneers heading into the wilderness from Detroit. Taverns like the Ten Eyck were located every few miles along the Territorial Road, providing food, drink, and rest. Conrad (apparently pronounced "Coon-rad") Ten Eyck was a larger-than-life character, and probably the source of the Wolverine nickname for Michiganders. Conrad joked with a little girl staying at his tavern that she was eating wolf meat, and she responded that she must then be a "wolverine."

Ten Eyck intrigued me because he was Dutch, as am I. But as I read about him, it soon became apparent that the boisterous proprietor of this Dearborn drinking establishment was on the opposite side of our common Dutch heritage. Ten Eyck was clearly from the 17th century New York side of the Dutch-American family, part of the profit-seeking settlers of New Amsterdam. My people, meanwhile, came to West Michigan later in the 1800's, around Holland and Grand Rapids, seeking religious refuge. Conrad was a dead ringer for his classmate and fellow New York Dutchman, former president Martin Van Buren—squat, wide-faced and bewhiskered. A bowler, not a basketball player. Instead of being squat like Ten Eyck, my Dutch family was all tall, part of the progeny that makes the Dutch the tallest people in the world. Maybe Ten Eyck's family left the Netherlands before they could consume much milk and cheese, which apparently accounts for the height of the Dutch. My strict puritanical ancestors, Dutch Calvinists, would also never have owned a tavern, providing spirits and damnation to travelers along the Territorial Road.

At 6'3", I fit the stereotype of tall Dutchmen. In other ways, however, I am an odd Dutch duck. The west Michigan Dutch were, and are, overwhelmingly conservative. When they emigrated from the Netherlands in the 1840's, they were actually a rare instance of a group of people leaving because their homeland was *too* tolerant. Perhaps the Netherlands today is so liberal because all the conservatives left the country and went to western Michigan and South Africa.

My extended Dutch family fits the conservative stereotype. I've joked that if I ever ran for political office, my mother might vote for me, but I probably couldn't get the support of cousins and aunts and uncles. A few liberal outliers tend to huddle together at family reunions for moral support—an ex-hippie Quaker cousin designing sustainable housing in Atlanta, another in a same-sex marriage, and a third doing Peace Corps-type work in Kurdistan. The other 95% of the family, though, is solidly in favor of small government and conservative social values.

While the Dutch imprint of moral rectitude was strongly imprinted on me, I tend to empathize with the underdog on economic and racial issues. I grew up in white suburbia, but Mayor Hubbard seems like an alien creature to me. I'm extremely proud, for instance, of the role Michiganders played in the Underground Railroad, and of our state's early stand against the death penalty. And only a pinko socialist would rather ride a bike than drive a car!

Growing up Dutch in west Michigan also meant a strict Calvinist point of view. My family's Christian Reformed denomination prohibited movies, dancing, and the teaching of evolution. Sundays when I was a kid meant no bike riding, no baseball, no TV, and no swimming in our backyard pool. Dad loosened up the rules in 1972, when he wanted to watch the Miami Dolphins win the Super Bowl. After that, we could watch TV after the evening church service. Yes. Two services, plus Sunday School and youth group. But even though the Sabbath was a day of rest, our parents did have us do homework on Sundays.

After examining the site of Ten Eyck's tavern, I rode my bike down Michigan Avenue and enjoyed a visit to the Dearborn Historical Museum. As a board member of the Morton House Museum in Benton Harbor, I wanted to stop at similar small museums on this trip. I wanted to learn about local history along the way, but also to see how other local history museums fare.

Visiting the McFadden-Ross House, part of the Dearborn museum complex, was like coming home to the Morton House. Their museum had a small gift shop to the left, just like ours, and both places had old bookcases and an unplayable piano. I conversed with the two Karens who were working in the upstairs archives. They recounted stories about Dearborn and we shared how our respective museums recruited board members and raised money. They told me about holding craft beer tastings, school kids churning butter in the old kitchen, and having teddy bear picnics. After a half hour of talking to the two Karens, David Tinder wandered in. This was a serendipitous treat. During his lifetime, Tinder compiled an amazing collection of Michigan photographs, which he donated to the Clements Library in Ann Arbor. I bought an autographed copy of the book about the Chicago Road that used his photographs.

Karen and Karen also shared stories of Dearborn's most famous resident, Henry Ford. As only the local experts can do, they revealed some behind-the-scenes dirt on Henry. They told the story of the night Ford died, when a major storm and flood occurred (Henry both came in to life and left it without electricity). One book, *The Secret Life of Henry Ford,* tells of Henry's secret boat trips along the Rouge River in back of his estate to meet his mistress. Perhaps I should be more respectful of a major historical figure like Henry Ford. However, I am a history teacher, so should I respect a man who famously said, "History is bunk"?

The museum, part of the Detroit Arsenal, was built in the 1830's, shortly after the Territorial Road was completed. The Arsenal's original mission was to "store, develop, manufacture, test, repair, and provide arms and ammunition" to what was then the western frontier. The McFadden-Ross Home was the original powder magazine, and wisely placed one and a half blocks away from the main complex.

It was afternoon, and time to make some progress down the Territorial Road. Michigan Avenue took me through Dearborn, Dearborn Heights (but I encountered no hills here), and Inkster. Detroit and its surrounding suburbs have some good bicycling opportunities, but this stretch of road was not bike-friendly at all.

In fact, Michigan Avenue here was an example of the worst of roads in America. Three lanes ran in each direction, with cars constantly whizzing by, and no shoulder or bike lane for me. Despite the wind, my orange Burley flag was continually bent sideways as cars and trucks blasted past.

I rode past mile upon mile of low-lying, low-quality business buildings. West 5 Auto Sales. Liberty Plumbing Supply. Mr. Outlet Furniture. A 7/11, with Taco Bell and a White Castle close by. Amy's Wig and Beauty Supply. Dollar Palace. Travel Log Motel. Mr. Smooth Café. Hydro Hut Hydroponics. As I rode down this visual nightmare, I sensed no planning, no architecture, no style or pride, little decoration. Perhaps this was a stretch of road where it would be better to be in a car, traveling too fast to really see my surroundings.

One moment of respite and history among the sprawl was a stop at the few remaining buildings of the mental institution known as Eloise. A couple of years ago, I had read *Annie's Ghost*, part of the "Great Michigan Read." *Annie's Ghost* was Steve Luxenberg's riveting memoir of a search for a long-lost relative who had been committed for most of her life to Eloise. I rode around the run-down buildings, looking in vain for the cemetery with many unmarked graves. Luxenberg gives a nice history of Eloise and its connection to the Territorial Road:

"By 1828, the Superintendents (of the Poor) were searching for a site to build a new and larger poorhouse, and Superintendent Ammon Brown urged them to consider land near his home in rural Nankin Township, nearly a day's ride from the city center, on the main stagecoach route between Detroit and Chicago. In early 1839, the Superintendents agreed, buying 280 acres and the Black Horse Tavern, a log cabin on the property that served travelers on the Chicago Road. The single story tavern became the Keeper's quarters, while the inmates of the first County House found themselves in a hastily constructed addition. But not all the inmates—in fact, not even most of them. 'Records show that 35 persons were transferred,' Clark's history reported, 'while 111 refused to go to that *awful wilderness*'."

I spent a few minutes in that awful wilderness, pretending to rest in the tavern and pondering whether my family and friends might commit me to a mental institution for going on this trip.

I was getting discouraged by this stretch of road until I got to Wayne. Here Michigan Avenue split into two one-way streets, with an actual downtown. It featured a venerable, renovated movie theater, the State Wayne Theater, advertising new reclining seats. I continued the luxury of stopping at every historical marker. One in Wayne indicated the 1824 Johnson's Tavern, which had been another stopping place for pioneers on the old Territorial Road. Johnson later sold the tavern to Steven G. Simmons. One night Simmons got drunk, murdered his wife, and became the last person in Michigan to be executed. I'm proud to live in the state that was the earliest in the Western world to outlaw capital punishment, in 1857.

It was also time for a late lunch, and serendipitously, the U.S. 12 Bar and Grill appeared on my right. It was named after the road I was following, and it also had bicycles parked out front. Two of the bikes belonged to a wonderful couple, Denise and Rudy, who were grabbing a bite to eat and drinking a beer. They saw my trailer and invited me to join them at their table. They lived in Detroit ("West-siders") and were on a bike ride out to Metro Airport and back. Denise, who was white, and Rudy, who was black, talked about living in Detroit and the vibrant biking community there. We discussed how the early roads were originally paved for bicyclists. "Detroit is coming full circle—going back to bikes," Denise said. It was a delightful encounter with these two like-minded people.

A couple of miles past Wayne, I crossed over the north-south I-275, which seemed to be the demarcation line of metro Detroit. On the other side, I encountered expansive vistas of greenery and open space for the first time. Canton, the community that stretched westward from I-275, was bike-friendly, if inadvertently. A nice wide lane, intended as a breakdown lane, served wonderfully as a 15-foot wide bike lane.

As I rolled along, I reflected on why I was doing this trip by bicycle. I wanted to see the Territorial Road, and for viewing, being on a bike is just the right speed. Since a car zooms along too fast, you often snap your neck back trying to get a glimpse of that Victorian mansion, or deer, or gardens of hydrangeas. Walking is too slow, unless you are one of those strange 21st century people who has patience. But a bicycle is just the right pace for taking in visual attractions while still actually getting somewhere. Tracing the Territorial Road by car would be a three hour trip—and would completely miss the point. Tracing it by foot would be almost a month—(and wouldn't happen, at least by me). I also hoped to interact with people along the way. A guy on a bicycle with a trailer is intriguing, whereas a guy with a backpack might be suspicious. A guy in a car is invisible.

Another reason for the bicycle is that while I don't like to go fast, I like the sensation of going fast. I don't think I've ever had my car speedometer over 90, but riding, just above the ground, in a go-kart at 20 miles per hour is exhilarating. I love to swim in a calm lake, partly because as I look to the side to breathe, eyes just at water level, it seems like I am racing across the surface. The bike is the same. Eighteen miles an hour down a slight decline is a thrill on a bike. Plunging down a steep hill at 26 miles per hour on a bicycle is a more amazing sensation, for me, than hitting 93 miles per hour plummeting down the Millennium Force roller coaster at Cedar Point.

A few more miles led me into the city of Ypsilanti, named after a famous Greek general from the early 1800's. I tried to visit the local historical museum, but a power failure had it closed.

At a coffeehouse in downtown Ypsilanti, I met James Mann, a local historian. Over coffee for him and a smoothie for me, James shared some of the many Ypsilanti stories he has collected over the years. Among these were "The Battle of the Toll Road" and "The Battle of the Cowsheds," neither of which resulted in anyone dying.

Later I found that I had missed a section of the Territorial Road. Just east of Ypsilanti, I should have taken Geddes Road north of the city. At Sheldon's Corners, the Territorial Road split off from the Chicago Road, which bends south at Ypsilanti to a route through the most southern tier of Michigan counties, dashes through the Irish Hills, and on to Sturgis, Niles, New Buffalo and ultimately to Chicago. The Chicago Road was the earliest road across Michigan, and perhaps more historic than my Territorial Road. But the Chicago Road did not lead home.

Ypsilanti was also a momentary hiccup in the trip, as a band holding my bike computer sensor on the wheel broke. I had already learned on this first day that the bike computer was a critical part of the trip, letting me know how far I had come and enabling me to figure how far the next stop was. The speedometer also kept motivating me to keep the pedals turning at a decent speed. The computer included a thermometer, which seemed to be recording how I was feeling, rather than the actual temperature. It was recording a temperature in the 90's, which is how I felt. My orange trailer flag hung limply and had a sheen of sweat. Temperatures were actually in the 70's.

Ypsilanti Cycle had not yet locked the door at two minutes after their closing time, and they graciously (and without charge) put a couple of zip ties on to hold the computer. For bike guys, however, they were not very interested in my trip.

Then it was on to my overnight stopping point, Ann Arbor, about 10 miles from Ypsilanti. Washtenaw Avenue, the road from Ypsilanti to Ann Arbor, is a busy commercial strip. My Ann Arbor contact, Jan, warned me, "Do not, do not, do not ride your bike on Washtenaw!" James Mann, back in Ypsilanti, told me, "Taking Washtenaw by bike is not recommended." Another contact said she did not even drive her car on Washtenaw.

So, of course, I rode my bike on Washtenaw. My orange flag was blown sideways again.

Washtenaw Avenue was a high-traffic, four lane road with a turning lane. There was no bike lane or any space at all. Cars had to slow down behind me until they had room to move into the next lane. But this stretch of road was a higher-class version of the road through western Wayne County, with Barnes and Noble instead of Dollar Palace.

I made it safely to Ann Arbor, despite car horns and stress. This was the route of the Territorial Road, and I was compelled to be historically accurate, if not completely safe.

Before stopping for the night, I rendezvoused in Ann Arbor with a high school classmate, Michelle. I never knew Michelle that well as a teenager. She was a girl, and so it was unlikely that an athletic nerd like me would have much interaction with her. We had gotten back in touch through the human connection marvel that is Facebook. Michelle was leading the liberal fight on Facebook, posting about social justice and the dire threat of Donald Trump.

After riding an extra mile past my turn and another mile back, my orange flag spinning, we met and talked on an elementary school playground. Her spirited adopted daughter from Ethiopia climbed on the ropes and bars with her friends. Michelle was a good representative of Ann Arbor, clearly the most liberal place in Michigan.

Most of those liberals were there as a result of Ann Arbor being home to the University of Michigan. The University of Michigan was one of a string of higher education institutions along my route. Earlier in the day I had gone through the campus of Eastern Michigan

University (originally Michigan State Normal School) in Ypsilanti. Before that was the University of Michigan-Dearborn campus, which featured a nice mural of Ten Eyck in the lobby of the administration building. Later in my trip I would pass Albion College, Western Michigan University, and Kalamazoo College. Those early Michigan settlers along the Territorial Road obviously knew the state needed some learnin'.

Apparently a controversy surrounds the naming of Ann Arbor. One story holds that the town was named for the wives of the two founders, Ann Allen and Mary Ann Rumsey. More likely, though, is that it was named just for John Allen's wife Ann, with the arbor appendage chosen "to describe the setting of sunshine and shadow produced by the scattered oaks in the 'opening.'"

It was time to stop for the night. Since the Mortons and other pioneer families may have slept under the stars as they traveled the Territorial Road, I did the same. I pitched a tent in the backyard of my friends, Lori and Scott. Lori was a friend from my sojourn during the Reagan years in Washington, D.C. In a sense, we were both fighting corporate America. I was helping my liberal U.S. Representative boss fight against Ronald Reagan's tax cuts for business. Lori was protecting historic properties from the greedy clutches of business developers.

We lived in a group house, two guys and two women on three floors of a Capitol Hill town house. I was making $18,000 a year, and Lori probably not too much more. Sharing expenses was the only way for 20-something singles to afford D.C., especially only four blocks from the U.S. Capitol building.

Lori and I and others in our group of friends and acquaintances lived the idyllic life that was essentially college without any homework—touch football on the Washington mall, *Moonlighting* watch parties, weekend bring a six-pack parties, dancing at local clubs, and scoring free food at political fundraisers. Lori was a social connector whom everyone loved and wanted to hang out with. She went on to be an uber-successful mom, and continues to make our world better as the executive director of the Northville, Michigan Downtown Development Authority.

It was a cool, calm night, with grilled chicken and wonderful conversation on the porch. I felt sure we were reenacting a scene similar to those in taverns and houses along the Territorial Road so many years ago.

Day Two
Wednesday, June 24
Ann Arbor to Albion

Ann Arbor's Dangerous Rock—No Girly Garmins—Lima's Twinkie—Chelsea to Grass Lake—Jackson: Republicans and Prisons—Ghost Towns—Bad Roads and Good Roads Earle—Albion's Rock.

The next morning, I had breakfast and more conversation with Lori. A missed opportunity at the Broken Egg Café proved to be my second biggest regret on the trip—only on the way out of café did I discover that they served the Elvis breakfast—peanut butter and banana French toast. Then Jan, from the Washtenaw County Historical Society, guided me through their museum, which featured a photography exhibit. (I loved the 1800's version of photoshopping—"headless portraits," where people posed with their heads seemingly on the table next to them). We also discussed biking. He was helping with PALM (Pedal Across Lower Michigan), which on this day was heading across Michigan in the opposite direction of me. A short

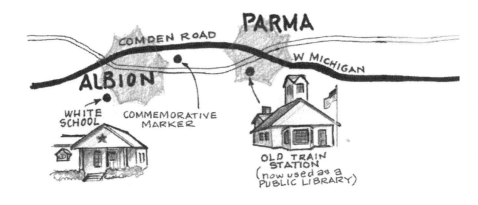

PARMA

COMDEN ROAD

ALBION

W MICHIGAN

WHITE SCHOOL

COMMEMORATIVE MARKER

OLD TRAIN STATION
(now used as a
PUBLIC LIBRARY)

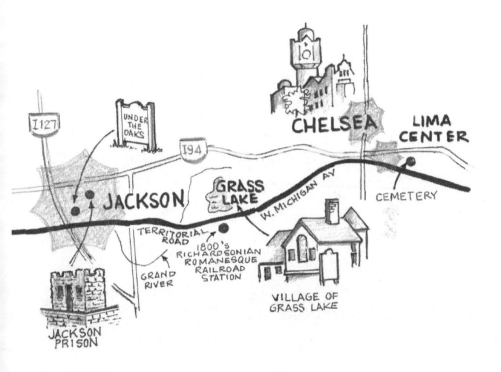

I 127

UNDER THE OAKS

I 94

CHELSEA

LIMA CENTER

JACKSON

GRASS LAKE

W. MICHIGAN AV

CEMETERY

TERRITORIAL ROAD

1800's RICHARDSONIAN ROMANESQUE RAILROAD STATION

GRAND RIVER

VILLAGE OF GRASS LAKE

JACKSON PRISON

49

distance from the museum, I wandered through Ann Arbor's hip, urban scene—taking in a farmer's market and the famous Zingerman's Deli.

Then it was out West Huron Street to Jackson Road, the local names for the Territorial Road here on the west side of Ann Arbor. I was searching for a boulder. This rock was the first of a number of boulders marking the Territorial road. My trip coincided with the centennial of these boulders, most of which were placed in 1915 or 1916. Glaciers brought the granite boulders to Michigan from Canada. A speaker at a boulder commemoration called the rocks the "first immigrants to the United States."

The prime mover behind placing these granite sign posts was the Daughters of the American Revolution. The DAR was formed in 1890, spurred by both the inspiration of the centennial of George Washington's inauguration, and the snub of being excluded from the Sons of the American Revolution.

From its inception, the DAR has been a leader in historic preservation. When the first transcontinental highways were being planned and built, a group called the National Old Trails Road Association was created. They wanted these first truly national roads to follow historic trails like the Cumberland Pike, Boone's Lick

Road, and the Santa Fe Trail. This association teamed up with the DAR to place commemorative boulders and plaques along these historic roads. Their purpose was, in the words of one member, "to study trails and post roads as they recorded the steady march of civilization from the East to the West."

DAR chapters in Michigan recorded that steady march at various points on the Territorial Road, with boulders in Ann Arbor, Marshall, Albion, Battle Creek, Kalamazoo, Keeler, and Benton Harbor. I felt the DAR ladies were kindred spirits, celebrating old places and trails and trying to preserve their memories. Not much physical evidence remains of the Territorial Road, and it was always a bright spot in the trip to come across a commemorative DAR boulder.

The Ann Arbor rock, originally located where the Territorial Road split from the Ann Arbor--Dexter road, was placed there in 1922. The Daughters of the American Revolution provided the tablet and the Sons of the American Revolution the boulder. The boulder was "a splendid specimen about ninety percent granite and weighing, as near as can be estimated, five tons."

Scott, the night before, had mentioned that he thought the boulder was no longer there. Jan from the Historical Society thought it had been removed also, but didn't know where it was located now. I worked my way through construction, and arrived at the original spot, which has a Marathon gas station next to it. I got off my bike, and met John, an older mechanic who looked like he had been around a while and might know something about a historic boulder. John certainly did know about the rock. Apparently, it had been hit by a motorist, who then proceeded to sue the city, the county, the Michigan Department of Transportation, and the Daughters of American Revolution. According to John, the suit was still in court. In the aftermath of this incident, the boulder was moved about ½ mile farther west to the corner of Maple and Jackson. I biked down the road and visited the boulder at its new site, now a safe fifty yards from the road.

Ann Arbor's Territorial Road boulder,
now in a safe place

On the western edge of Ann Arbor, I went under I-94, encountering the interstate for the first time since Dearborn. It was here that the scenery definitely changed. The area from Detroit through its western suburbs, and on through Ypsilanti and Ann Arbor, constitutes a small megalopolis. From this point on, though, the terrain would be rural, interspersed with small cities surrounded by suburbs. An early pioneer traveling on the Territorial Road in the 1830's noted a similar change here:

> "Ann Arbor was at the extreme west of the habitable world, beyond which the sun went down into a boundless, bottomless morass, where the frightful sound of yelling Indians, howling wolves, croaking frogs, rattling massaugers, and buzzing mosquitoes added to the awful horror of the dismal place."

Perhaps the current residents of metropolitan Detroit still have similar thoughts about the rest of Michigan. Possibly they think like Big Apple residents do in that famous *New Yorker* cartoon that shows everything west of the Hudson River as a vast wasteland.

On the other side of I-94, a wonderful thing awaited—a bike lane. After a few miles, the sign said, "Bike Lane Ends," but I still had a four-foot paved shoulder all the way to Chelsea. The day was also in the 70's, with almost no wind. My second day on the route of the Territorial Road was a perfect day for biking. I enjoyed a sunny morning of biking, unperturbed by the traffic and sprawl of yesterday. Did the Mortons encounter similar beautiful days as they walked alongside their wagons?

To navigate my way along the Territorial Road, I did not have much more technology than the early pioneers. The Mortons and other travelers on the road probably did not have a map. Finding their way was mostly just following the path through the woods. The occasional tavern would also have been a source for wayfinding, if necessary.

For my wayfinding, I had a paper map—up-to-date, but considered old-fashioned today. I had bought a detailed "DeLorme's Atlas and Gazetteer," with one inch equaling 2.54 miles. I tore out the seven relevant pages to make a lighter load to bring along.

I could have used GPS, but I am both a technophobe and a directions snob. While I have adopted technology at home and in the classroom, I am convinced that many technologies are empty addictions or impediments to developing our natural abilities. My friends at school often term me "nearly Amish."

Directional technology aids, like Garmin or TomTom, seem especially invidious to me. Guys, in particular, are supposed to know where they are going. It is simply unmanly to sit in a car and be told by a robotic woman's voice which way to turn.

In addition, I am overly proud of my sense of direction. (As Daniel Boone once said, "I can't say as ever I was lost, but I was bewildered once for three days.") I do have an "inner compass." I constantly, and unconsciously, keep track of which way is north relative to which way I am headed. A distant relative, Ronald Jager, discusses this phenomenon in *80 Acres,* a book about growing up in rural Michigan. He makes the case that people in the Midwest have a better sense of direction because of the north, south, east, west lines set up by the Land Ordinance of 1785. He says:

> "...there are two kinds of people, those who have an inner compass and those who do not. To have an inner compass is to have, for example, a ready answer to the question, Which way *seems*

north? Those lacking an inner compass have no intuitive answer; they can only contrive one. Put another way, those with the compass have a mental quirk by which the back of their mind is always busy noting directions, making corrections, generating constant low-level interest and information about north-south-east-west. They may not always be right about directions, but something always seems right. In contrast, those without a compass can move for days, even through unfamiliar places, entirely heedless of directions; normally they simply don't care about them. People with an inner compass do care; for them the difference between north and east has a vividness like the difference between left and right. They want to have what *is* north also *seem* north; so they work at it...I am aware that readers of these observations may find them provocative if they have an inner compass—and somewhat peculiar if they do not."

As I grew up in southwest Michigan, my environment was oriented around those consistent Land Ordinance lines. When I looked out my bedroom window or the window of history class, I knew I was looking north. My Midwestern inner compass was locked in place from an early age.

So no girly Garmin for me. On this trip, I occasionally looked at my map, knew where I was going, and set out in a manly way. (Except, of course, the beginning of this trip, where I went the wrong way.)

Between Ann Arbor and Chelsea lies Lima Center (pronounced like the bean, not the Peruvian city), a crossroads not even big enough to be called a hamlet. Here were two interesting items—a cemetery and Twinkie. The cemetery was just before Twinkie's house. It caught my eye and made me circle back. I have a fondness for old cemeteries. It is one of the few ways that we can really connect with the past. A cemetery is a permanent (I hope) remembrance of past generations, more concrete and real than genealogy charts and old photos. I've told my wife that I have few requests for when I die, but I need a granite tombstone. (As the owner of a monument company once told me, "Granite lasts for 1,000 years, or your money back.") Just as I have wandered cemeteries searching for my ancestors, I hope one day far in the future that my distant descendants will discover my final resting place.

The Lima Center cemetery was away from the road between two hayfields and up a rise. I parked my bicycle near some trees that might have been here in the 1830's and wandered around the old graveyard. Some of the weathered tombstones marked the graves of men and women who were some of the early travelers down the Territorial Road.

Twinkie, whose real name is Florence, was the current proprietor of a centennial farm and 1885 farmhouse just down the road from the Lima Center cemetery. Twinkie was on her riding lawn mower as I pulled into her driveway. Her house is the style known as Upright and Wing, a folk style of architecture that came to the Midwest with migrants from New England. A welcoming bench sat under the porch along the front. The old stones along the road were topped with a replica vinyl white picket fence. Two towering old maples shaded the front of the handsome house. The classic red barn surrounded by blooming day lilies proudly sported a green sign designating it as a centennial farm.

Twinkie got off to talk and tell me about her farm, which was settled by her great-great-grandfather,

William Green Beach, in 1853. Her grandfather was a four-star general, and a great-uncle died in the tragic Bataan death march of World War II. Her father remembered the Territorial Road being paved around 1920. She and her family were obviously proud and protective of the homestead. This feisty woman regaled me with stories of winning legal battles against the power companies, land agents, and the township supervisor.

Twinkie's 1853 Homestead

Another quarter mile brought me to the center of Lima Center, dominated by a late 1800's interurban train station with a four-story tower. I got out and talked for a few minutes with the current occupants, who run a home health care agency. The Detroit, Ypsilanti, Ann Arbor and Jackson Railway built this unique brick station in 1901. Interurbans were a sort of light rail commuter system, popular in the early 1900's. The conspiracy theory is that General Motors engineered their demise to sell more cars.

I biked on a few more miles, and over to the north side of I-94, where I stopped for a chimichanga in Chelsea. One of Chelsea's fame claims is actor Jeff Daniels, who still lives in Michigan and started the Purple Rose Theater in town. As a history teacher, my favorite of Daniels' many film roles is as Colonel Joshua Chamberlain in the movie *Gettysburg*. On a family trip to the battlefield at Gettysburg, my son Sam and I pretended to fix bayonets and charge down the slope of Little Round Top. Instead of Confederates at the bottom, we confronted a pair of porta-potties.

Chelsea is also known as the headquarters for the Chelsea Milling Company, which makes Jiffy mixes—still one of the best deals in the grocery store. You can go on a factory tour, which includes getting a free box of corn muffin mix at the end.

Chelsea has a vibrant downtown, replete with distinctive restaurants, artsy shops, and bookstores. Apparently, it is much improved from the mid-1800's, when this comment was made: "It is said there is but one girl in Chelsea who owns a tooth brush and she combs her eyebrows with it." However, downtown Chelsea was just off the route of the Territorial Road, which beckoned me onward.

Another 10 miles on a beautiful afternoon rolled by, mostly countryside. When I stopped to eat a Clif Bar, I saw on the map that the town of Grass Lake was up ahead. I had two thoughts on my sunny, warm bike ride: can I swim in Grass Lake, and does it have an ice cream shop? A friendly guy edging his sidewalk gave me directions to both. A swim in the cool water, and a Twister (it would be a blizzard at Dairy Queen) made Grass Lake one of my favorite places on the Territorial Road. It didn't hurt to have a rebuilt 1800's Richardsonian Romanesque railroad station across the street to block the sun while I ate my ice cream.

Cooled and satisfied, I set out west once again. The city of Jackson, the county seat of Jackson County, was 10 miles farther on. In the 1830's, President Andrew Jackson took some time away from killing the National Bank and removing the Native Americans to set up and name the counties of Michigan. As one 1800's Michigan politician put it, President Jackson "took occasion to write the names of himself, his vice president, members of his entire cabinet, and the territorial governor, conspicuously and indelibly on the

61

map of Michigan." These became known as Michigan's "Cabinet Counties." After leaving Jackson County, I would be riding through Calhoun County (Jackson's Vice President), Van Buren County (Jackson's 2nd Vice President), and Berrien County (named after Jackson's Attorney General). Nearby Cass County was named for Lewis Cass, the Territorial Governor at the time, and later President Jackson's Secretary of War. One of Andrew Jackson's final acts as President was to end the territorial government of Michigan and make it a state.

"If there is a dreary spot upon the face of the earth, it is inside the walls of the Jackson prison."

Just a few blocks north of the Territorial Road in downtown Jackson is another early accomplishment of the newly-formed Michigan legislature. The state decided they needed a prison, and located it in Jackson. Shortly after the Territorial Road went through town, the prison opened in 1838. Most prisoners were in for larceny. Apparently the original wooden walls were ineffective, as 20% of the prisoners, including the only murderer, escaped in 1839.

In 1900, 20-foot high stone walls were constructed, which still stand and look both formidable and creepy at the site near downtown Jackson. One of the early buildings is the Armory Arts Village, now studios and apartments for artists. Tours, complete with living history guides, can be taken through the old prison.

The stone walls of old Jackson prison

Travelers can also tour the newer version of the Jackson State Prison a couple of miles north of town. The Cell Block 7 Museum is a fascinating look inside the largest walled prison in the world, which covered 57 acres and held 6,000 prisoners.

As I entered the visitors' parking lot, the concertina razor wire surrounding the prison caught my eye. After paying the entrance fee, I entered the holding cell. Although I knew I could walk out, it was a bit eerie looking out from behind the bars. The entry area also had a visitation room with a postcard-size window to look through, and mug shots of inmates on the wall (oddly with suits and ties), and a strip search area.

The main cell block is an enormous open hall with five levels of cells on each side. Cell Block 7 once held 561 prisoners at a time. I walked into the cells, which featured only a single bed, toilet, and bulletin board. A retired corrections officer was describing daily life in the prison to a dad, his daughters, and their grandmother. I checked out displays of homemade (jailmade?) confiscated weapons.

A video showed scary Warner Pathe newsreel footage of the 1952 riot at the prison. Prisoners took over the facility, held guards hostage, and burned buildings. The riot was one of a series of nation-wide prison riots in the early 1950's.

The museum also had exhibits on prison industries, including a farm ("Home Grown" brand canned goods), furniture-making, and of course, license plates. Another interesting exhibit portrayed the 1975 escape of an inmate via helicopter. He had an accomplice hijack a private helicopter, which made a quick landing in the prison yard and then dropped him off outside the prison walls a couple of miles away.

Just before I left, the retired guard/docent electronically opened a whole floor of cell doors. Then they were closed with that classic and ominous clang that meant a loss of freedom for those behind the bars. I was thankful I could simply walk out into the fresh air and sunshine.

Alonzo Vincent served as the warden of Jackson prison from 1901 to 1906. Vincent was also prominent farther west down the Territorial Road, running both the local Republican Party and hotels in St. Joseph and Benton Harbor. In the Civil War, he was a member of the Western Sharpshooters and participated in Sherman's March to the Sea.

As the warden at Jackson, Alonzo Vincent was perhaps the kind of thinker we need today. According to one early 20th century writer, under Vincent "a new era of treatment was opening," and that Warden Vincent believed in "the value of unshackling the mind of a convict." He apparently believed in treating prisoners as human beings, and most notably abolished the flogging pole at Jackson. This was part of the mentality that made Michigan a prominent state in the Progressive Party movement. Unfortunately, Alonzo Vincent might not recognize our current legislators who have recently dismantled the Great Lake State's progressive legacy.

A few miles north of the Territorial Road near Jackson is the grave of Holling C. Holling. (Yes, that was his name.) Holling wrote one of my favorite childhood books, *Paddle to the Sea,* which perhaps inspired this trip. This treasure of a book traces the journey of a small carved Indian in a canoe from a stream flowing into Lake Superior, down through Lake Huron, past Detroit, into Lakes Erie and Ontario (and over Niagara Falls), through the St. Lawrence Seaway, and out into the Atlantic Ocean. I dreamed of being that little Indian in a boat traveling around Michigan.

I wandered off the Territorial Road in downtown Jackson, looking for history. With some help from a friendly young Jackson city employee, I found one of Michigan's claims to fame: the birthplace of the Republican Party. There are some who claim that a city in Wisconsin is the birthplace, but those people are just wrong. Here, "Under the Oaks," a convention met to voice its opposition to the Kansas-Nebraska Act and to form the GOP. According to Charles Moore in *History of Michigan,* "the convention adjourned to a beautiful oak grove that covered a tract of land known as 'Morgan's Forty,' where a platform was hastily built and draped with the stars and stripes. Among the sturdy oaks, under the free blue sky the Republican Party was born that day." There are still some big oaks here, although I can't vouch that they were here in 1854.

"Under the Oaks"
Birthplace of the Republican Party

There was also some irony here. Andrew Jackson was one of the main founders of the rival Democratic Party. And here in the inner part of Jackson's city, it was unlikely that many of the residents of this block voted Republican in the last couple of elections.

I left the oaks under the free blue sky and rejoined the path of the Territorial Road. On the west side of Jackson, I encountered my one and only unpleasant encounter of the trip. One owner of the road yelled, "Get your ass on the sidewalk where it belongs!" The misguided soul could not have known that it was oxen I was impersonating, not a donkey.

Six miles west of Jackson, I stopped at a crossroads originally known as Sandstone Village. According to the *Combination Atlas Map of Jackson, Michigan,* "Sandstone Village at one time bid for to rival Jackson, and in 1837 it had two hotels, a bar, and quite a number of stores, but those 'wildcat' days of speculation passed away, and the Village of Jackson, rapidly increasing in population, left Sandstone out in the cold, and the disappointed speculator soon gathered up his effects, and left for more remunerative fields." I can confirm that Sandstone is no longer a thriving metropolis. It did have a thriving church, though— the Sandstone Congregational Church, which was just finishing feeding 190 people at a Swiss steak fundraiser. I tried to mine for some historical information among the committed faithful who were cleaning up, and also made my most regrettable decision of the trip—I turned down apple pie. My orange Burley flag pointed longingly back toward the uneaten pie as I left the parking lot.

It was about dinner time, and just west of here would be my projected 40 miles of bicycling for the day. It was a stunner of a day, though, and rain was projected for the next day, so I decided to push on into the evening. I also didn't have friends or family to stay with on this stretch of my journey. If it were up to me, I was tempted to just find a place to duck into the woods and pitch my tent. Maybe it was about this spot that the Mortons made camp for the night back in 1834. That, however, meant I would either panic my wife or lie to my wife. I didn't want to do either, so she made a reservation for me in a hotel. Hey, even the pioneers sometimes paid for overnight accommodations. Days Inn today or local tavern in the 1830's, I figured it was pretty much the same thing.

A few miles west of Jackson, I bicycled into the small town of Parma. Michigan Avenue, the route of Territorial Road, turned left here. I turned right and rode down the three blocks of Main Street. It was easy to see how Parma was once a thriving place, with two-story Italianate commercial buildings, boasting tall windows with rounded tops. The mill that brought farmers to town was still there, as well as the Michigan Central train station that brought freight and visitors. A weathered sign hanging on the depot's side read:

Detroit | Parma | Chicago
36 | | 198
miles | | miles

Parma's train station along the Territorial Road

It was also easy to see that Parma is a good example of the death of small towns in Michigan and across America. When the main road between Detroit and Chicago went right past here, and the Michigan Central Railroad still picked up passengers, Parma was a happening place. But when I-94 was built about 1960, modern America passed by places like Parma. While the old Parma used to employ people at the mill along the tracks, now the only possible job was at the gas and convenience store at Exit 134. Nothing in Parma drew visitors. It was a bit of a ghost town as I rode through.

The one place I saw some life was the old interurban train station, today a fine example of adaptive reuse as the town library. I ran into Barbara the librarian as she came out at closing time. We talked a bit, and she gave me a couple of peppermint candies for energy for the road.

Next, I expected to go through Albion, but I had now gone about 50 miles— by far the most I had ever ridden in one day. A local Albion historian, to the detriment of his town, wrote that originally Territorial Road did not dip south into Albion, but continued straight west and on past the city. It sounded good to me at that point.

The Territorial Road was known as Comden Road at this point, and as I came over a rise I saw that I was now a long way from the big city of Detroit. Before me was the first gravel road of the trip. It also went up a steep hill, with soft sand mixed with the gravel. Dust caked my now less-orange flag. I came close to being discouraged, almost getting off my bike and walking a stretch for the first time. But I struggled up the hill, and then saw that the gravel road only lasted for about ½ mile. The next stretch was the finest pavement of the whole trip—fresh, satiny-smooth asphalt. It didn't even look like anyone had driven on it yet; there were no cars in sight. It was all mine!

Unfortunately, that beautiful pavement only lasted two miles, whereupon the famous potholes of Michigan resumed. (We were recently named as the state with the worst roads in the United States.)

Michigan's roads are notoriously bad these days, but we still have it much better than the pioneers on the Territorial Road. Stories of the rough roads abound from those early days. Writers spoke of the "fearful and horrible roads...leading out of Detroit in 1833 to 1837." Mud was often so bad that wagons would sink to the box of the wagon. Famous writer and traveler Harriet Martineau traveled through Michigan in the 1830's. She spoke of having to get out of the wagon and walk, experiencing such "hopping and jumping; such slipping and sliding; such looks of despair from the middle of a pond; such shifting of logs, and carrying of planks, and handing along the fallen trunks of trees."

Breakdowns were common. A writer in 1836 said, "The road from this to Ypsilanti looks at certain times as if it had been the route of a retreating army, so great is the number of wrecks of different kinds which it exhibits." When stage coaches ran, a standing joke was told about meeting a mud hole: "First class passengers remain seated, second class get out and walk, third class get out and push." Joseph Woodman, a settler near Paw Paw, related his experience with the Territorial Road: "I landed at Detroit in the spring of 1835, and made my way to Kalamazoo, though mud and mire, with two teams, a span of horses and a yoke of oxen, and I often had to double up my teams in order to get through. I frequently met stages, with the passengers on foot, carrying rails or poles with which to pry the vehicles out of the mud holes."

Some of these were money-making mud holes. Land or cabins often sold for a higher price because it was adjacent to a troublesome hole. The proprietor of the mud hole was happy to help free, and fleece, the traveler.

Roads in Michigan and across the nation began to be improved in the 1890's, and bicyclists were responsible. The advocate in Michigan was the wonderfully-named Horatio "Good Roads" Earle. Earle, who was president of the League of American Wheelmen, said, "I often hear now-a-days, the automobile instigated good roads; that the automobile is the parent of good roads. Well, the truth is, the bicycle is the father of the good roads movement in this country." Horatio achieved great results in leading the good roads movement, becoming the state's first highway commissioner and overseeing the paving of the first concrete highway in America (Woodward Avenue in Detroit). He also advocated, in 1901, the interstate highway system that was built in the 1950's and 60's.

Unfortunately, a good majority of Michiganders didn't want good roads at that time. "Nobody wants good roads but the bicyclist," was an old quote. Most people were farmers, who thought the roads were good enough for their horses and wagons, and definitely did not want to pay more taxes. (Today, people in Michigan don't think the roads are good enough, but they still do not want to pay more taxes.) Farmers could substitute working on the road in lieu of paying cash for their taxes. "Each team, wagon, plow and man would count a day's work, and any present-day labor union would have been pleased with the extremely short sessions of the farmers each forenoon and afternoon on the job, with committee meetings under a shade tree and in fence corners every half hour, more or less."

An account of this 1890's battle said that the bicycle movement "was a force beating against a stone wall of indifference and even bitter antagonism on the part of many taxpayers. To numerous good citizens the bicycle was anathema, and in many localities a good-roads advocate was about as popular as an abolitionist in the ante-bellum South."

I was just north of Albion. Where the road splits to detour into Albion lay the largest commemorative boulder of the trip. The arrow-shaped ten-ton piece of granite towered over me. Amazingly, the boulder was found in a nearby farm field. This boulder was dedicated by the D.A.R. on July 30, 1915, so I was within a month or so of the centennial of this stone.

Later, I found a picture of the dedication. The old photograph shows a crowded scene, with both buggies and Model T's. An American flag is partly draped over the freshly-unveiled rock. Somewhere in this scene were four original pioneer ladies who traveled the road in the late 1830's.

The 1915 dedication of the Territorial Road commemorative boulder, north of Albion

Because of perfect riding weather and a forecast of rain the next day, I had gone 57 miles on this day. I was tired and within a mile of my hotel when I went by an older woman out in front of her home, a converted one-room schoolhouse. The friendly owner, Dorothy, was out weeding her garden as I pulled up with my bicycle. Her home, the White School, was probably built in 1860. She told me about her ancestor, A.J. Phillips, who invented the adjustable window screen. She also invited me in to see the interior of her lovely home. Her house was immaculately clean, with a grandmotherly décor of Americana and knick-knacks. I had to squint my eyes deeply to imagine the classroom full of pioneer kids hard at work on their lessons.

One more mile brought me to my modern tavern, the Days Inn motel, with junk food available next door. I was a tuckered traveler when I settled in for the night.

This was the halfway point of the trip. I had gone 100 miles. Over the two days, I had a riding time of 8 hours and 37 minutes. My average speed was just over 11 miles an hour.

Day Three
Thursday, June 25, 2015
Albion to Battle Creek

Marvelous Marshall—Taverns along Territorial—The Original Potawatomi Path—The Red Man's Rebuke—Finding Truth— Underground Travelers—Pondering Race—Prairies and Oak Openings

As expected, the next morning was rainy, but it was a gentle rain, with no wind. I barely noticed the spattle of small raindrops against my orange flag. A mile or so down the road, Comden Road was cut off by I-94, so the road detoured around and over the interstate. On the other side, where the road was truncated, a homeowner had set up a basketball court on the abandoned part of Territorial Road. I turned right, off to the west once again.

Eight rainy but pleasant miles down the road brought me into Marshall, named after John Marshall, who was Chief Justice of the U.S. Supreme Court from 1800-1835. (Marshall often battled with Andrew Jackson, the namesake of the city east of here.) An early pioneer account remarked, "In reality it was named after

77

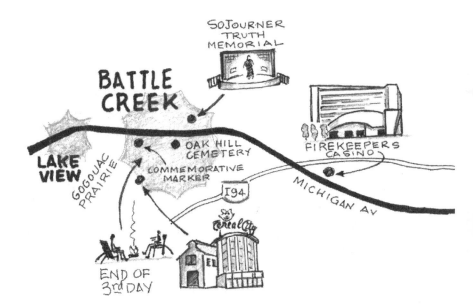

SOJOURNER TRUTH MEMORIAL

BATTLE CREEK

FIREKEEPERS CASINO

LAKE VIEW

GOGOUAC PRAIRIE

OAK HILL CEMETERY

COMMEMORATIVE MARKER

I94

MICHIGAN AV

Cereal City

END OF 3rd DAY

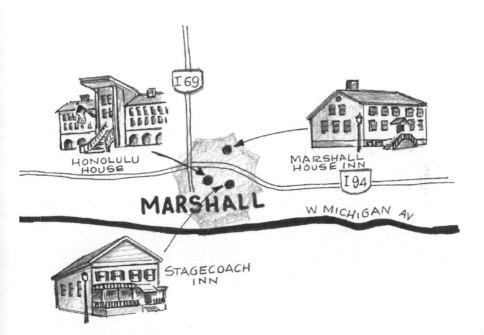

I 69

HONOLULU
HOUSE

MARSHALL
HOUSE INN

I 94

MARSHALL

W MICHIGAN AV

STAGECOACH
INN

the Chief Justice, but most people supposed it to be a transposition of all marsh."

I knew Marshall would be a great place when I saw that the town has 40 historical markers and 11 museums. History seems to be working for Marshall. It has a lively, thriving downtown, with art galleries, specialty shops, and charming local restaurants. Each fall, thousands of visitors show up for one of the best home tours in America.

Many residents of the Michigan Territory thought Marshall was going to be the state capitol—the people of Marshall certainly thought so. They laid out a Capitol Hill area, and there is a governor's mansion here. According to a 19th century Calhoun County history, "Ann Arbor was to be assigned the university, Jackson the penitentiary and to Marshall the capitol was assigned."

I started my Marshall meanderings by meeting with an engaging tour guide, Susan, at the Honolulu House. I was happy to get out of the rain for a tour of a singular old house. Abner Pratt, a former ambassador to the Sandwich Islands (now Hawaii), built the Honolulu House in 1860. The Honolulu House was modeled after the Royal Palace in Hawaii, but ultimately is a Gothic/Italianate/Hawaiian mash-up. While living in the

Honolulu House during Michigan winters, Ambassador Pratt continued to wear tropical clothing. He caught pneumonia and died. "There's no bad weather, only inappropriate clothing."

Susan's tour was a non-stop combination of local history (Marshall was founded by Sydney Ketchum, a land speculator who followed the Territorial Road in 1830), stunning design details (a one-of-a kind chandelier with hunting scenes and trompe l'oeil doors), and unexpected items in the Honolulu House (a Swiss music box with bird songs and a portable organ for home funerals).

Marshall thrives today because it has preserved so much of its history. Susan shared with me that at one point the Honolulu House was run-down and abandoned. Standard Oil wanted to tear it down and build a gas station. On my trip down the Territorial Road, I saw plenty of towns and cities that were unappealing and languishing because they had torn down most of their history. They did have gas stations, though.

Marshall had the third boulder of the trip marking the Territorial Road, but the first dedicated, in 1912. Like the markers in Albion and Battle Creek, it was "Dedicated to the Pioneers of Calhoun County."

One of the 40 historical markers in Marshall told the story of Sam Hill, as in the old saying "What in the Sam Hill is going on here?" a euphemism for some stronger language. Sam, who retired in Marshall, surveyed the Upper Peninsula of Michigan, which is some rugged country, and apparently called for some proper cussing. A Google search gives six or seven possible alternative origin stories for the Sam Hill expression. But since this story is told by a marker on the Territorial Road, it is clearly the true one.

Another marker on the way into town commemorates the Crosswhite Affair. The log cabin of runaway slave Adam Crosswhite and his family stood just a few yards north of the Territorial Road in the 1840's. In 1847, his owner from Kentucky came looking for him, and enlisted the local law to help him arrest Adam and his family and return them to the South. Instead, the good people of Marshall stood up to injustice. They formed a mob to protect the Crosswhites, and compelled the local authorities to arrest the Kentucky slave catchers (man-stealers, they were called back then) instead of the runaway slaves. The Crosswhites were then able to escape to Canada, going the other way on the Territorial Road. Actions like these across the North led to the Fugitive Slave Law, which made it easier to return runaway slaves and compelled northerners to assist slave catchers. Widespread northern opposition to this law was one of the roots of the Civil War.

The Crosswhite Affair is the kind of event I use to try to inspire my students to take action to combat injustice in the world. One of my proudest moments is when I stood up at a meeting to protest the unjust suspension without pay of one of my colleagues. Although I, along with others, spoke just a few words, that action made a difference. I wish there were more opportunities in life to stand up for justice.

While previous taverns on my journey on the Territorial Road were now empty spots marked only by historical signs, Marshall had two taverns still standing. I rode my bike over to the National House Inn, a tavern since 1835. Barbara, the proprietor, has been running it as a bed and breakfast since 1982. She showed me some of the historically-authentic rooms and talked about the tavern's history, including the building serving as a possible spot on the Underground Railroad, complete with an underground room. I then had a great burger in the Stagecoach Inn, located in a historic Greek Revival building on the former Territorial Road.

These taverns along the road provided the early pioneers a bed for the night, food, drink, directions and some needed socialization. They might even have some fun. An early account said of a tavern stay, "How wonderful it is to dance with girls who have never known a corset." Here, in Marshall, I finally had some sense of the places the original pioneers stayed. It is certainly possible that the Morton family stopped here on their way west.

If they did stop, here and at other taverns, it may have influenced their hospitality when they settled at the end of the Territorial Road in Benton Harbor. Their first home in Benton Harbor was a stopping point for many travelers who spent the night before crossing the river on their way to St. Joseph to sell crops or buy household goods for the return trip. Later, when the Mortons built their hilltop house in 1849, it became known as the Indian Hotel. The Mortons offered their front porch to Native Americans traveling to Lake Michigan.

After lunch, I set off in some light rain towards Battle Creek. On the way I passed the huge and busy FireKeepers Casino, run by the Nottawaseppi Huron band of the Potawatomi tribe. I'm sure none of the gamblers thought about this road as a former Indian path as they turned into the parking lot. It does seem an appropriate spot to put a Native American casino.

Territorial Road, like most other pioneer roads, followed the paths of Native Americans, in this case the Potawatomi. The Indians, in turn, had merely followed the paths of buffalo that once lived this far east. In *Paths of the Mound-Building Indians and Great Game Animals,* part of the Historic Highways of America series, Archer Butler Hulbert says,

> "It was for the great game animals to mark out what became known as the first thoroughfares of America. The plunging buffalo, keen of instinct, and nothing if not a utilitarian, broke great roads across the continent on the summits of the watersheds, beside which the first Indian trails were but traces through the forests. Heavy, fleet of foot, capable of covering scores of miles a day, the buffalo tore his roads from one feeding-ground to another, and from north to south, on the high grounds; here his roads were swept clear of debris in summer,

and of snow in winter. They mounted the heights and descended from them on the longest slopes, and crossed each stream on the bars at the mouths of its lesser tributaries...until the problem of aerial navigation is solved (Hulbert wrote in 1902), human intercourse will move largely on the paths first marked by the buffalo."

When the Territorial Road was built and the Morton family was making its way past this future casino site, the Potawatomi numbered about 2,500 in Michigan. Their lands stretched from southern Michigan into northern Indiana and Illinois, wrapping around Lake Michigan into Wisconsin. The coming of white settlers like the Mortons, down pioneer roads like the Territorial Road, spelled doom for Potawatomi sovereignty in Michigan. They lost their land in a series of land cessions between 1807 and 1833. Forced removal of the Indians happened between 1835 and 1840. While the southeastern part of the U.S. was the scene of the infamous Trail of Tears, the Potawatomi were removed in a similar action known as the Trail of Death. Instead of Oklahoma, the destination of the Potawatomi was Kansas. (John Brown's famous raid, as part of Bleeding Kansas, took place on the banks of Potawatomi Creek.)

Not all of the Potawatomi, however, ended up west of the Mississippi. Chief Leopold Pokagon led a group of Potawatomi that resisted removal, and their descendants live in Michigan to this day, just north and south of the Territorial Road. In addition to buying land, the Pokagon Band was apparently able to stay in Michigan partly because they were Catholic. The Catholic faith was a legacy of the French missionaries and voyageurs who settled in southwestern Michigan in the 17th and 18th centuries. Leopold Pokagon testified to his Catholic faith in a request to Father Gabriel Richard to send his people a priest:

> "Father, Father, I come to beg you to give us a Black-gown to teach us the word of God. We are ready to give up whiskey and all our barbarous customs. Thou dost not send us a Black-gown, and thou hast often promised us one...An American minister wished to draw us to his religion, but neither I nor any of the village would send our children to his school, nor go to his meetings. We have preserved the way of prayer taught our ancestors by the Black-gown who used to be at St. Joseph. Every night and

morning my wife and children pray together before a crucifix which thou hast given us, and on Sunday we pray oftener. Two days before Sunday we fast till evening, men women and children, according to the tradition of our fathers and mothers, as we had never ourselves seen Black-gowns at St. Joseph."

The "American minister" Pokagon refers to was a Protestant minister, (probably an advocate of removal) and one historian argues that Leopold Pokagon, by converting his band to Catholicism, successfully created a distinctive identity for his people. Father Richard would be proud.

Leopold's son and successor as chief of the Potawatomi was Simon Pokagon. Simon Pokagon shook hands and visited with Abraham Lincoln at his inauguration. At the 1893 Chicago World's Fair, he was an important part of what was known as the Columbian Exposition. As a representative of Native Americans, he seemed to alternate between two attitudes towards whites. On one hand, he was the guest of honor at Chicago Day, and he presented the mayor of Chicago a deed for the land on which Chicago was built. In his speech, he said, "The red man is your brother, and God is the father of all."

Later, he presented a contradictory view by issuing a booklet called *Red Man's Rebuke*, a fiery attack on the treatment of Native Americans:

> "In behalf of my people, the American Indians, I hereby declare to you, the pale-faced race that has usurped our lands and homes, that we have no spirit to celebrate with you the great Columbian Fair now being held in this Chicago city, the wonder of the world. No sooner would we hold the high joy day over the graves of our departed fathers than to celebrate our own funeral, the discovery of America. And while you who are strangers, and you who live here, bring the offering of the handiwork of your own lands and your hearts in admiration rejoice over the beauty and grandeur of this young republic and you say, "Behold the wonders wrought by our children in this foreign land," do not forget that this success has been at the sacrifice of *our* homes and a once happy race."

Both the Nottawaseppi and Pokagon Bands began a return to tribal identity during the New Deal under the Indian Reorganization Act of 1934, and they were granted sovereignty in the 1990's. Both bands have built successful casinos. While many white Americans are resentful of these Indian casinos, they seem a good example of positive karma. After all the wrongs that were done to Native Americans, casinos seem to be some historical redemption.

I bicycled through more rain in the afternoon on the way to Battle Creek. The name would suggest a creek-side conflict that gave this city its name, but barely. Battle Creek was "named for a ruckus between two Indians and two surveyors, one of the world's most miniscule Indian affrays, in which no wounds worse than a broken head were inflicted."

As I came into Battle Creek, I followed Michigan Avenue, which runs right into downtown. Most of the way across the state, I followed this main road. However, I had read a passage in the book celebrating the centennial of Battle Creek (1831-1931) that "the old Territorial Road did not pass through the present Battle Creek. It branched off from what we now call the Marshall Road, at a point east of the city, and went through Goguac Prairie." Local superstar historian Berenice Lowe, who wrote *Tales of Battle Creek*, had tracked down the mystery of the original route of my road through Battle Creek. Her investigations showed that the original Territorial Road deviated from Michigan Avenue and cut south of downtown. This was a difficult stretch of the road to trace. The old road, according to Berenice, today is blocked by the C.W. Post cereal plant. On the other side of the plant, I zigzagged down streets that were now at crazy angles to the original path of the road.

This was also the closest I came to dying on the trip, as I nearly turned in front of a car. The driver and I slammed on our brakes. Both my orange Burley flag and I quivered momentarily as the driver steered around me. Perhaps my head was still back in the 1800's, when traffic was not so much of a concern.

Berenice's path led me to the back (and locked) gate of Oak Hill Cemetery. I detoured a couple of blocks around to the front gate, climbed up the hill to the back gate, and then zigzagged again through the cemetery, trying to follow the general path of the Territorial Road without riding over graves.

The early path of the Territorial Road seems to go right past the grave of a famous American and a resident of Battle Creek, Sojourner Truth. Her marker says:

IN
MEMORIAM
SOJOURNER
TRUTH
BORN A SLAVE IN
ULSTER CO., NY
IN THE 18TH
CENTURY
DIED IN
BATTLE CREEK,
MICH.
NOV 26 1883
AGED ABOUT
105 YEARS
'IS GOD DEAD'
S.T.

Sojourner Truth's grave in Oak Hill Cemetery,
Battle Creek

My fascination with Sojourner Truth increased when I learned that she spoke English with a Dutch accent. Truth was a former slave owned by Dutch New Yorkers. I then crossed the Kalamazoo River, and took a detour downtown to visit the wonderful memorial to Sojourner Truth, where I held hands with the twice-as-large-as-life statue of Truth. We were certainly an improbable Dutch couple.

The Sojourner Truth memorial in downtown Battle Creek

Recent efforts to put a woman on the $20 bill have centered on Harriet Tubman, but perhaps Sojourner Truth would be a more worthy honoree. Truth was a slave in New York state, and after she gained her freedom, became a well-known spokesperson for the abolitionist movement before the Civil War. However, she didn't stop there.

She strongly advocated women's rights, recruited black soldiers in the Civil War, (her son was a member of the 54th Massachusetts, the *Glory* regiment) worked for land for former slaves (40 acres and a mule), came out against capital punishment, and sought prison reform. And she predated the actions of Rosa Parks by 90 years, riding whites-only streetcars in Washington, D.C. in protest.

She lived the last twenty years of her life in Battle Creek, first in the spiritualist community of Harmonia west of town, and then later on College Street downtown.

Near the Sojourner Truth memorial, in a beautiful riverside park, is a striking monument by sculptor Ed Dwight commemorating the Underground Railroad. It struck me at this point that while I was traveling from east to west, this was approximately the route, in the opposite direction, of runaway slaves in the 1840's and 50's. The route of the Underground Railroad in Michigan came up from Indiana to Vandalia and Cassopolis in Cass County, then north to the route of the Territorial Road to Battle Creek. These places had settlements of Quakers, the strongly abolitionist group that also attracted Sojourner Truth to live in Battle Creek. From here, runaway slaves moved eastward to Marshall, as evidenced by the Crosswhite affair and perhaps that hidden room in the National Inn. Then the route led to Jackson, which makes it an appropriate place for the birthplace of the Republican Party. Republicans, though, including Abraham Lincoln, were no abolitionists.

In Ypsilanti, I had visited a small park that included tributes to Elijah McCoy, the local African-American inventor (origin of the phrase, "the real McCoy"), and also Harriet Tubman. Harriet's statue is a good reminder that Ypsilanti was a stop on the Underground Railroad, but not a good local history marker, since she never came to Michigan but rather was a conductor in Maryland and Pennsylvania. The start of my bicycle trip, Detroit, was the final goal of runaway slaves.

Even before I left from Campus Martius, I checked out the Underground Railroad monument on the banks of the Detroit River. This fine sculpture (also by Ed Dwight) shows a family of runaway slaves, including a mother holding a sleeping toddler, looking and pointing across the Detroit River to their final freedom destination, Canada. I didn't go across the river to

Canada, but Windsor has a companion sculpture showing an escaped slave with raised arms of exultation and praise.

When we talk about the Underground Railroad in my U.S. History class, I try to emphasize the local connection to Michigan. It is also one of my irrational teacher fears that a student may leave my classroom thinking that the term Underground Railroad was literal, not figurative. That is, they might think it was actually a railroad beneath the surface of the earth—like a subway line from Kentucky to Canada.

It is also difficult to prove that many places were actual sites on the Underground Railroad. Like Al Capone hideouts in Southwest Michigan (another popular obsession of my students) an Underground Railroad station back then was something they wanted to keep secret. Today, it would make a great tourist stop.

Riding my bicycle down the Territorial Road afforded me time to think about issues like race in our society. The origin of my views on race is a mystery to me. Where did my feelings on race diverge from my fellow Dutch in South Africa, my fellow Dutch in western Michigan, and from my neighbors in suburban Stevensville?

Like most Americans, I grew up in a segregated community. My suburban neighborhood was 100% white, and the only African-Americans lived in Benton Harbor, an economically-depressed city about seven miles away. My earliest encounter with a black person was when my brothers and I tormented the African-American housekeeper/nanny next door. This included an episode where we knocked on the door, sprayed her in the face with squirt guns, and ran off.

What may have started to change my outlook was attending Kalamazoo College, a small liberal arts school with a divided mission—partly turning out pre-med majors and partly social justice warriors. I can't say I was too involved in saving the world at this point. The only protest in which I participated was against rising tuition costs. I spent most of my time playing basketball and having fun; but perhaps the social justice mission of K College rubbed off on me.

As a newly-graduated political science major, I headed off to Washington, D.C. to save the world (at least from Ronald Reagan). While living there for three and a half years, I had my first significant contact with African-Americans.

I was hired as a legislative assistant for U.S. Representative Alan Wheat from Kansas City, who was one of the few African-American congressmen elected by a majority-white district. Wheat was a relaxed, easy-going guy who connected personally with staffers. The first weekend after I was hired into his office, Congressman Wheat showed up on the Washington Mall to play touch football with the staff. I worked daily in an integrated office.

I found a house to share with some fellow Michigan friends on G Street in the northeast section of DC. A block away was H Street, the site of the 1968 riots following the assassination of Martin Luther King and still an economically depressed area. Our next-door neighbor was Houston, the African-American co-pilot on Air Force Two, the Vice-President's plane. I was the only white guy in the pick-up basketball games at the playground down the street.

I also played basketball on a wonderful team of both black players and white players who competed in various leagues and tournaments. Tony Upson, the African-American principal of Theodore Roosevelt High School in northwest D.C., assembled the team.

As I gradually lost interest in politics and thought more about becoming a teacher, I volunteered for the Higher Achievement Program (HAP). Every Monday night, I would venture into Anacostia in southeast

Washington to help at-risk African-American students with writing and math.

Then I left Washington and went home to Michigan to be a teacher. I lived at home with my mother for a couple of months. As a move of independence, I not only got my own apartment, but also my own church. I joined First Presbyterian Church on Morton Hill in Benton Harbor, located right behind the Morton House. Martin Luther King once said that 10 a.m. on Sunday morning was the most segregated hour in America, but First Pres was an integrated church with both black and white members. After a fire in 1980, First Presbyterian thought about moving to the suburbs like so many inner-city churches. However, led by dynamic and charismatic minister Dirk Ficca, First Pres made racial reconciliation its mission.

Going to church on Morton Hill led to me living on Morton Hill. A renovated early 1900's Victorian, the Sowers House, had been fixed up by a couple of guys, and was for sale at a typically low inner-city price. The house, with 2,500 square feet and a beautiful wrap-around porch, would have cost four times as much had it been across the river in St. Joseph. So, in 1995, I bought the house and became what some people termed a "pioneer" in a mostly black neighborhood. In 1997, I married Mary Jo, and we lived there (adding two kids along the way) until 2005. Even though many of our white friends and family were shocked, our neighbors were great, and we never had any problems living there.

As a history teacher living two blocks away from the Morton House Museum, it was perhaps inevitable that I would end up volunteering and being on the Board of Directors there. The Morton House Museum was run by a mostly-white group, almost all ladies, with the purpose of displaying the home of a white family. The surrounding neighborhood and city must have thought of us as this strange, alien museum without any connection to them.

In the past, the Morton House Museum was just a house museum, with period rooms, antiques, and stories about the Morton family. In recent years, however, the Morton House Museum has changed its mission to be "The Home of Benton Harbor History." Instead of just telling the story of a white pioneer family, the museum seeks to tell the whole story of Benton Harbor, including the modern-day experiences of African-Americans in this city.

Back on the road, I detoured through downtown. Battle Creek was also part of the 1890's bicycle craze.

The Battle Creek Bicycle Club formed in 1896. One of the best riders, reportedly, was a fellow named W.K. Kellogg. He, of course, started some cereal company, but more important to me was that he was a fellow bicyclist. Kellogg commuted to his office on an "old, tall-type high wheeler bicycle." He was one of the first in Michigan to sign up as a life member of the League of American Wheelmen, just behind Horatio "Good Roads" Earle.

Then it was back to Territorial Road, which from here, for the first time on the trip, uses the original name. It starts at Riverside Drive and goes west, but I backtracked east for 500 yards down an overgrown path to the edge of the river. Here was a part of the road I could imagine being very much like the old road, with the wilderness close on each side.

The Territorial Road rises from the river here. And does it rise! This was the toughest hill of the trip. My thighs burned as I pushed mightily to get my wagon up the hill. I imagined that my orange trailer flag was bent to a 45 degree angle. Heavy panting might have echoed the labored breathing of the Morton family oxen in 1834 as they went up this hill just outside of Battle Creek. I could imagine Eleazar at the reins, with his wife Joanna Morton (dressed in a bonnet) shouting encouragement to the pair of oxen as they slipped and struggled up the steep, muddy road. The older Morton boys—Charles, Henry, William and George--would have jumped off the wagon as it began to slip in the mud. (I'm sure it was raining the day they went up the hill as well.) One of the boys would have grabbed the halter and helped to pull the team along up the steep grade. The other boys would have pushed on the tailgate of the wagon, as the girls jumped out to lighten the load. The rain would have been pelting down as the oxen nearly gave up and began to slide back, just before a final, strained push pulled the wagon over the crest of the hill.

With this bit of historical insight, I guess my struggle with bike and Burley up this hill wasn't so bad.

At the top, where the oxen and I recovered, lay the edge of the Gogouac Prairie. It would have been a dramatic sight for the Mortons and other pioneers as they conquered the hill.

Much of Michigan in the 1800's was covered with forests, but occasionally the pioneers came across these prairies—vast open stretches of grassland, and treeless. Seeking farmland, these prairies were paradise. No trees to clear! Most of us are dedicated tree-huggers today, but back then trees were obstacles. The prairies were the most desirable land for these early pioneers, the first acres claimed at the local land office.

The prairies here in Michigan were not natural. The Native Americans created and maintained them through regular burning. Long before Europeans came to America, huge chunks of the eastern continent were open prairies like these. European immigrants have the idea that the frontier was heavily wooded because 90% of Indians were killed by disease, dramatically diminishing the burning that was done.

In addition to the Gogouac Prairie, there was the Climax Prairie southwest of Battle Creek. Farther west, near Schoolcraft, was the granddaddy prairie of them all, Prairie Ronde. It was "praised as the most beautiful spot in the world," one historian noted. "In the center of the grassy plain stood a large "island" of timber, and within the "island" a lake."

The other pleasing geographical feature the pioneers came across was known as "oak openings." These were savannas, with just burr oak trees spread in the grass lands. James Fenimore Cooper wrote a book about this area of West Michigan called *Oak Openings.* According to one pioneer,

"The annual fires burnt up the underwood, decayed trees, vegetation, and debris in the oak openings, leaving them clear of obstructions. You could see through the trees in any direction, save where the irregularity of the surface intervened, for miles around you, and you could walk, ride on horse-back, or drive in a wagon wherever you pleased in these woods, as freely as you could in a neat and beautiful park."

The landscape dubbed by the pioneers as "oak openings" was open woodland in which the trees were sparsely scattered over a grassy surface. An 1834 account by a traveler going inland from Detroit well describes this landscape.

"The monotonous landscape ceases near Ann Arbor; and here the country became more interesting as one approaches the high plateau. The dense forest disappear and lakes surrounded by pretty hills and park like woods, which the Americans call 'oak openings,' meet the traveler's eye... where the trees stand a few paces apart and where the ground is overgrown with luxurious grasses. Passage is obstructed neither by bushes nor by fallen trees."

The Battle Creek commemorative boulder for the Territorial Road was along this stretch of the former Gogouac Prairie, so I stopped and paid homage. The boulder was in the side yard of a beautiful brick Italianate mansion, probably built in the 1870's or 1880's.

Battle Creek's Territorial Road boulder, atop
Gogouac Prairie

The rain for the day was stopping just as I was. I rode my bike a few more blocks. At the corner of Territorial and 28th Street, my eight-year-old nephew and godson Ben waited. He rode his small bike side-by-side with me to my father-in-law's house. He was excited to be part of his uncle's adventure. He helped me hose off the Territorial Road from my bicycle and we ate dinner.

We went out to Battle Creek's Bailey Park to watch my other nephew Zach's baseball doubleheader. I spent a pleasant warm summer evening alternating between watching Zach scoop low throws at first and Ben chase foul balls into the parking lot. Then it was back to my father-in-law's house. I got trounced in pinochle before pitching my tent and camping in Pa Smith's backyard, once again like the Mortons and other pioneers. My bicycle and Burley, with the orange flag, were parked safely in a comfy garage.

Day Four
Friday, June 26, 2015
Battle Creek to Paw Paw

Fort Custer Detour—Small Town Heroes—Michigan's Main Street—
Lincoln in Michigan—College Memories—A Fateful Wind—A Paw Paw
Pause

With my bicycle, orange flag, and me cleansed of yesterday's rain and mud, I set off again west on Territorial Road through the southwestern part of Battle Creek, an area known as Lakeview. I was only able to go half a mile before two obstacles to tracing the old road stood in my way: the Battle Creek airport and Fort Custer Training Center, a military base. Perhaps I was too passive, but I didn't give much thought or effort to obtaining permission to pedal across the major runway of the airport. On the other side of the airport, the maps showed a tantalizing route through Ft. Custer, a major military training base that is home to about twelve different military units. In the wake of 9/11, I wasn't optimistic that they would let me ride through the base. Master Sergeant John Marietta, though, was

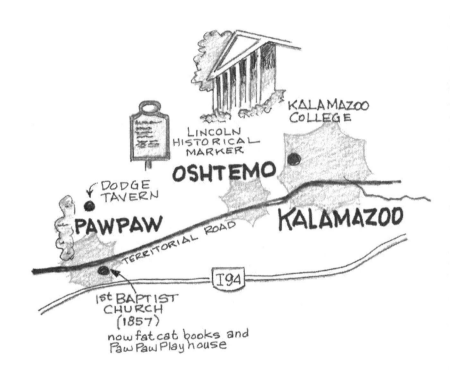

KALAMAZOO
COLLEGE

LINCOLN
HISTORICAL
MARKER

OSHTEMO

DODGE
TAVERN

PAWPAW

TERRITORIAL ROAD

KALAMAZOO

I94

1st BAPTIST
CHURCH
(1857)
now fat cat books and
Paw Paw Play house

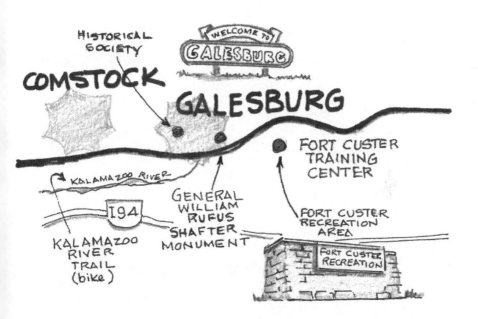

HISTORICAL SOCIETY

WELCOME TO GALESBURG

COMSTOCK

GALESBURG

KALAMAZOO RIVER

I94

KALAMAZOO RIVER TRAIL (bike)

GENERAL WILLIAM RUFUS SHAFTER MONUMENT

FORT CUSTER TRAINING CENTER

FORT CUSTER RECREATION AREA

FORT CUSTER RECREATION

most accommodating about the possibility, but not on this day.

"No way," he said. There was a major training exercise going on, and no chance of riding through. So I set off on Dickman Road (named for a local World War I general), which paralleled Territorial Road to the north.

On this road in the 1850's was a small village called Harmonia. It was established by Spiritualists, who believed in the ability to contact the dead through mediums. Rare was the séance that was well-done by the medium. Sojourner Truth bought a lot and built a small house here in Harmonia, before moving into downtown Battle Creek.

I then rode through Ft. Custer Recreation Area, a favorite spot for our family camping trips. Each summer, my wife's extended family gathers here for a long summer weekend. We pitch tents and park trailers together, and share campfires and family memories. My two sons and their cousins experience a full-on weekend. They rise early to fish out of Grandpa's small boat in Jackson Hole or Eagle Lake. Late mornings are for the boys and me to tackle the Fort's amazing mountain bike trails. Some are just around and through the trees fun, while others are "technical," meaning plenty of rock and log obstacles. On the challenging hills, we do "biking and hiking," where we have to get off our bikes and push them up the inclines. The most amazing trail is "Trenches," where we ride in and out of old World War I training trenches. After lunch, all the generations head to the Eagle Lake beach, featuring uncles throwing and dunking nephews in the water. A potluck cookout is next, followed of course by smores and card games.

On this quiet morning by myself, I took a break from the road to swim in the shimmering waters of Eagle Lake. The water continued the cleansing of my old life, and I emerged from the lake with a renewed sense of purpose to finish my journey and start my new venture.

Riding through the campground, I went around a park gate and followed an abandoned paved road. At the end of the road, I picked up a path through the woods that bordered the Territorial Road, just on the other side of the military fence. I plowed through the vegetation, stopping only to take a picture of the foundations of an old homestead, and to serve up a robust meal to mosquitos. This felt more like an Indian footpath, as it would have been before the Territorial Road was built. I finally burst out on Ft. Custer Drive, with a padlocked gate barring me from the section of road that I could not ride that day.

A mile or two down Ft. Custer Drive brought me once again to Michigan Avenue, now the road running through Galesburg. One of the pioneer families who came down this road in 1833 was the Mortons, who stayed in Galesburg for a year or so before moving on to the western end of the Territorial Road in Benton Harbor.

I pedaled into town and turned left into the Galesburg Historical Museum, connected to the local library. Waiting for me at the door was Kay Maxon. Kay was a long-time insurance agent. He and his office were at the very heart of town. Besides being on the museum board, Kay was the last of the Galesburg Lions Club and had formed a special non-profit organization to keep the local Boy Scout troop going. The tools from his grandfather's Galesburg blacksmith shop were displayed inside the museum. Kay was a piece of Galesburg history, and works hard to keep that history alive.

Kay brought me into the museum. Consulting some old local maps, he helped me trace my route through the area, and then walked me through the museum and through the history of Galesburg. It is a valuable documentation of small town life in America.

"We have lots of stuff," he told me with an easy, loud and genuine laugh. The museum was packed to the gills with hand-made maps, flags, family and school pictures, and household implements. My favorite Kay joke was when he showed me the bedroom with the water jug and chamber pot. "It's a baseball bedroom...you have the pitcher on the dresser, and the catcher under the bed."

The museum seemed to be a two-person effort, with Kay and a former schoolteacher named Keith Martin doing much of the work. ("I'm into flags, and Keith is into railroads," Kay said.) They get by on donations and sales of Keith's talks on DVD. It reminded me of the struggle I'm part of with the Morton House— not enough volunteers, time, or money. I tried to help the effort by buying a DVD and making a small donation. Kay finished off a great visit by buying me lunch in downtown Galesburg.

Right across from the restaurant, at the very center of Galesburg, stands a fine monument to an overlooked figure in U.S. history. General William Rufus Shafter, born in Galesburg in 1835, rode dramatically through several periods of U.S. History. Shafter was decorated for bravery in the Civil War, where he also commanded African-American troops. He continued this role after the Civil War, where the black troops were known as "Buffalo Soldiers" as they fought in the Wild West against American Indians. Most prominently, he was the lead general during the Spanish-American War in 1898, capturing the main Cuban city of Santiago. He was, though, not happy about being overshadowed by Teddy Roosevelt and the Rough Riders—an early case of media bias, according to Keith Martin. In a Kalamazoo homecoming parade after the Spanish-American War, 75,000 people cheered Shafter. The local girls chanted, "Who are we after; Who are we after; We are after General Shafter!"

What intrigued me, though, was Shafter's style. According to Keith Martin, Shafter was "coarse, abrasive, gruff" and he "drank, gambled, swore to excess, and fought with his troops." Shafter weighed over 300 pounds and had to be carried on a door in the Spanish-American War. About that swearing—one historical account said that Shafter would "swear till the air'd pop and the breezes'd spit red fire."

The monument at the corner of Augusta Road and the former Territorial Road had a bust of Shafter, along with some metal from the U.S.S. Maine, the sinking of which led to the start of the Spanish-American War. ("Remember the Maine, and to hell with Spain!") The monument also had a history like the Territorial Road boulder in Ann Arbor. General Shafter (the stone version) was hit by a truck and flung 75 feet away. No word on whether there was any swearing during the accident.

My last decision in Galesburg might have been the best. I went next door to Young's Bakery and Deli and ordered a cronut (combination of croissant and doughnut). Although they had some already made in the case, the owner insisted on taking a few minutes and frying one fresh, dipping it in cinnamon and sugar. I ate it, still warm, a couple of miles down the road—perhaps the tastiest item I ate on the trip.

Between Galesburg and Comstock, I came across something new, and something that would prove to be unique on this trip—a bike trail separate from the main roadway. This was the new Kalamazoo River Trail, which stretches over 22 smooth asphalt miles between Galesburg and Kalamazoo. My orange flag curved backward as I sped along. Planners of this trail promise the day when riders can cycle across the state from Lake Huron to Lake Michigan on separate paths like these. I was truly torn when the trail deviated from the route of the Territorial Road. I chose historical authenticity over a smooth track (Eleazar Morton's wagon never had it that good), with a hope to return for some fun another day.

Michigan Avenue, past Comstock, took me into Kalamazoo. Here I missed a boulder. The DAR placed this boulder in 1916, but not on the Territorial Road. It marks "one of the two old trails over which the early settlers came into Kalamazoo County." Presumably Territorial Road was the other old trail, as this boulder was placed well north of my route.

Much of the Territorial Road from Detroit to Kalamazoo was known as Michigan Avenue. Remarkably, it was a 1920's novel that brought about this name. The Territorial Road, as it went through many downtowns, was previously known as Main Street. Sinclair Lewis wrote the best-selling book *Main Street* in 1920. It was a devastating portrayal of small-city life. Lewis' fictional city of Gopher Prairie showed a society of small-minded, provincial, boring and unprogressive people. As a result, it was suddenly unfashionable to have a Main Street at all. When Jackson was considering a name change in the late 1920's, some comments in the local paper were, "Main Street is a small town name," "Main Street is for a one-horse town," and "Main Street is a relic of other days." Instead, a chic and fashionable "Boul Mich" was envisioned, stretching from

Detroit to Chicago. Marshall adopted the Michigan Avenue moniker in 1924, Battle Creek in 1928, and Kalamazoo and Jackson in 1929.

I pedaled through a more thriving downtown than when I attended Kalamazoo College in the early 1980's, the renaissance seemingly led by craft beer. Some of the early founders of Kalamazoo were my fellow West Michigan Dutch, who put their wooden shoes to good use in raising celery in the muck, making Kalamazoo "The Celery City." (According to one source, the black soil was so mucky even the horses wore wooden shoes.) I walked my bike through the downtown Bronson Park, lined this day with food trucks doing a brisk business. This park also marked the spot of Abraham Lincoln's only appearance in Michigan. I've always felt a special connection to Lincoln since we are both the exact same height. For a Morton House event for the 150th anniversary of the Civil War, I grew a Lincoln beard. My wife sewed a historically-appropriate suit, and I recited the Gettysburg Address for the crowd. I'm disappointed Abe never rode a bicycle.

Lincoln wasn't in Jackson when the Republican Party was birthed "Under the Oaks," but he was certainly one of those galvanized by the possible expansion of slavery under the Kansas-Nebraska Act of

1854. Before this, he had left the government and was merely a country lawyer in Springfield. As Lincoln said, "I was losing interest in politics, when the repeal of the Missouri Compromise aroused me again. What I have done since then is pretty well known." The historical marker here in Kalamazoo notes that some who heard him speak in the park thought he was too conservative on the issue of race (that is, he was not an abolitionist). Lincoln would have been sympathetic to those escaping slaves sheltered in Battle Creek and Ypsilanti and who crossed the river in Detroit, and also to Adam Crosswhite as he escaped the bounty hunters in Marshall. He was certainly no abolitionist, however, and Sojourner Truth might have given him a piece of her mind had they met in Battle Creek. The remarkable thing about Lincoln, though, is that he evolved. The conservative on race in Kalamazoo in 1856 changed over time into the Great Emancipator of 1863 and the leader in the fight for the 13th Amendment outlawing slavery in 1865. Sojourner Truth and Abraham Lincoln did eventually meet, with Truth traveling from Battle Creek to the White House, where she said that "he was the best president who has ever taken the seat."

After reflecting on our 16th President, I got back on Michigan Avenue for a bit and stopped at my alma mater, Kalamazoo College.   While the University of Michigan was known as "the Harvard of the West," K College likes to be known as "the Princeton of the Midwest," complete with Princeton's orange and black colors.

I put down my kickstand at the bottom of the hill of the Quad. My orange flag bobbed cheerfully back and forth. I looked up the fair Arcadian hill, just as I did when I was 18 years old, at the most beautiful campus in Michigan. This idyllic spot still holds a strong emotional attachment in my heart.   These beautiful oak trees captivated me just as the "oak openings" must have for the pioneers on the Territorial Road—a temporary easy spot in the road.   My four years at K College were a protective cocoon where I played basketball and wandered through several social studies departments. It was a place where I didn't have to declare a major until well into my junior year. I hung out with friends, playing Frisbee golf around big oaks and through brick arches. I wrote articles for the school paper about the dean's former rock 'n roll life. I was a resident advisor at a place that wasn't all that interested in making students follow the rules. Although I ended up as a Political Science major, the most vivid and memorable classes for me were Basic Drawing and Creative Writing.   Our

"Annihilation Inc." flag football team dominated in the fall, followed by sledding down the Arcadian hill on cafeteria trays in the winter.

A return to my alma mater

In the spring, K College had, and has, a most wonderful tradition. Engraved in stone on the wall of my freshman dorm was the phrase, "The end of learning is gracious living." So each year, on the most beautiful sunny day in May, there was a surprise announcement in the morning that this day was "A Day of Gracious Living." Classes were cancelled for the day, and we were off to a Lake Michigan beach or waterskiing at a suite-mate's summer cottage.

I often dream of my college years in Kalamazoo. In these dreams, I am just on the periphery of the action, wanting but unable to go back. At the base of this Acadian hill, it was time to continue on down the Territorial Road. But my bright'ning face spoke of love for Kalamazoo College.

> O, Kalamazoo, our faithful friend,
> We offer thee a song,
> To praise the home where friendships blend
> and weld so true and strong.
> O, sacred refuge and most hallowed place,
> Where hope and joy renew,
> With tight'ning grip and bright'ning face
> That speak thy love, Kazoo.

All the way from Battle Creek to Paw Paw, I had the wind at my back. Had I looked back at my trailer flag, maybe it would have been pointing forward.

I never noticed.

The feeling of the wind at my back while on a bike is the feeling of nothing. Because I am riding at about the same speed as the wind, it just feels calm. It is a benefit, but a benefit that is easy to overlook. A pushing wind has to be really strong for a rider to notice it. But any kind of breeze in the face, no matter how gentle, is one you definitely notice. And a strong head wind is flat-out discouraging.   It is the same with a gentle downslope. I've often been out on a ride that I thought was simply flat. But when I turned around and headed back, lo and behold, the same route was uphill the other way.

It's often hard to recognize how grateful we ought to be.

Our society has been involved in a major discussion about white privilege, and it strikes me that this bicycling analogy might help us understand. For many white people, we live our lives in America with the wind consistently at our back. We never notice how privilege pushes us along, but it is there. We never notice how much of our lives are a gentle downhill ride. For others, especially African-Americans, life in America is a bike ride through life with the wind constantly in their face.   Sometimes it is a gale force wind. Sometimes the wind knocks you off your bike.

It was another 10 miles west to my next stopping spot for the night, Paw Paw.   Paw Paw didn't have a boulder, but it did have a historical marker with some interesting and amusing information about the Territorial Road:

"One of the three great east-west routes in pioneer days, the Territorial Road from Detroit to St. Joe tapped the rich lands of the second "tier" of counties. Approved in 1829, the road was not surveyed through Van Buren County until 1835. Although at first it was only a "blaze and a name," the route was soon teeming with emigrants and travelers. The Dodge Tavern in Paw Paw, a famed stopping point, was so crowded at times that some weary persons, old timers said, "offered a dollar for a post to lean on."

I stopped at Fat Cat Books, complete with a fat cat in the window. The friendly and helpful proprietor, Jean, explained the history of the building, which was originally the 1st Baptist Church, built in 1857. Besides the bookstore, it housed the Paw Paw Playhouse, featuring the Village Players. Jean, of course, sold the tickets. She took me upstairs to show me what had been the unusual second floor sanctuary, now the theater.

Paw Paw is also notable as an early 1900's site of a popular Chautauqua. The Chautauqua started in western New York state, and was a sort of summer adult education experience. Teddy Roosevelt called the Chautauqua "the most American thing in America."

Traveling Chautauqua companies, known as circuit, or tent Chautauquas, would bring in a week or two's worth of speakers, musicians, lecturers and entertainers. Most notable at the Paw Paw Chautauqua was three-time presidential candidate William Jennings Bryan (he lost all three times). Bryan was also in the national spotlight just before he died as one of the lawyers in the famous Scopes Monkey trial between evolutionists and creationists. Another appropriate speaker in Paw Paw, right near the Territorial Road, was Horatio "Good Roads" Earle, the early bicycle advocate and first state highway commissioner.

After Chinese food for dinner, I took a detour about three miles off the Territorial Road to stay with Craig Warner, a high school friend, at his and his wife's beautiful farmstead. Although they are not farmers, they have the classic red barn a few steps away from their restored farmhouse. Instead of cows or tractors, the barn has a half-court basketball floor. We shared a beer and reminisced about the good old days at Lakeshore High School. Craig and I were teammates on a magical 25-1 high school basketball team in 1979.

Basketball is the ultimate team game, and the magic was the coming together of a group of late-bloomers. Our All-State teammate was the manager of the freshmen team, and the rest of us rode the bench until our senior year. I was even on the junior varsity team as a junior. But the summer before our senior year, a bunch of just really good guys bonded into a tight-knit machine. We went from a mediocre program to one of the best teams in the state, riding a devotion to teamwork and defense. We ran off win after win in front of packed gyms of red-clad fans. Mike was the 6'5" shooter and rebounder, our best player. John was an energy guy who provided boards, points, and enthusiasm. Craig, known as Doc, came off screens to hit his deadly jumper. I provided passing and defense (I was labeled Chuck "Big D" Jager by the local newspaper). Harv couldn't shoot and couldn't dribble with his left hand, but was fast and wily. Harv was the best of us, charismatic and a born leader. He also had demons, tragically killing himself in his early 30's.

It was a marvelous journey of friendship and community, ending in a heart-breaking thumping at the hands of the best team in the state.

Craig and I sat in front of a roaring fire, thinking back to those best of times at Lakeshore High School. Then it was off to bed to rest and look forward to the last day of my trip.

Day Five
Saturday, June 27, 2015
Paw Paw to Benton Harbor

Tea Pot Dome—An Interstate Dream—Help on the Trail—More Ghost Towns—The Bicycle Craze—House of David—A Benton Harbor Comeback—Home to the Mortons—The Last Boulder—Back in Time Down Territorial—The Last and Best Stretch—Finding Bicycle Bliss

With clearing skies on the western horizon, I set out on my last day in a light but steady rain. The first three miles that morning were backtracking my last three miles from yesterday. I was going east, and against the wind. It seemed crazy, but this whole venture probably sounded crazy.

The Territorial Road west of Paw Paw is Red Arrow Highway, named after a Michigan National Guard division that played a significant role in both World War I and World War II. I stopped for a chocolate-chocolate-chip muffin at Teapot Dome, a friendly old-style breakfast and lunch stop. Over time, the place took the name of the restaurant. When the original owners opened in the early 1920's, the Teapot Dome scandal

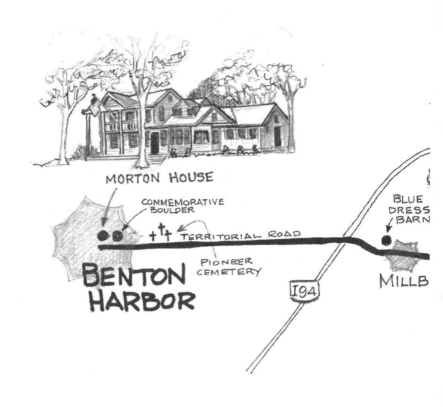

MORTON HOUSE

COMMEMORATIVE
BOULDER

BLUE
DRESS
BARN

TERRITORIAL ROAD

PIONEER
CEMETERY

BENTON
HARBOR

194

MILLB

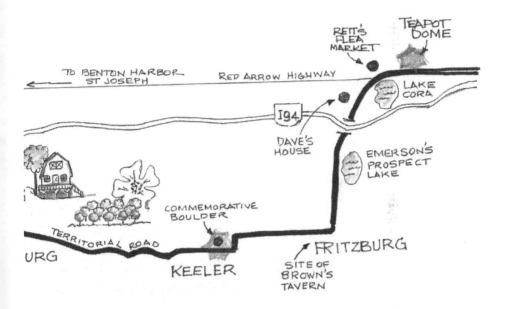

was in the news. This was the boring oil lease corruption scandal of the Warren G. Harding administration (clearly the best Presidential middle name ever—Gamaliel), not the juicy Clintonesque scandal we learned about later. So how did the name of a 1920's scandal in California become the name of a place in Michigan? One newspaper account quoted a descendant of the original owner of the diner, who said, "Grandfather liked the sound of it."

At Lake Cora, the road bent southward and is still known today as Territorial Road for the last 40 miles to Benton Harbor. I turned off Red Arrow Highway at Reits' Flea Market (the largest in Michigan, according to the sign, but not very busy on this rainy Saturday). Along this stretch, the Van Buren County Road Commission erected signs marking the Territorial Road, noting its start in 1829. As I photographed one of these, a man named Dave came out of his house, mentioning he saw me on the news the night before! We talked for a few minutes and I continued on my way.

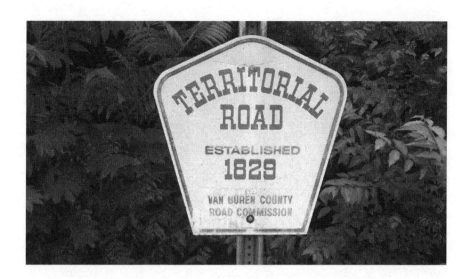

The road began to travel back in time. It became a country lane, then a gravel road. There were woods, and a lake, and I saw deer and egrets. A bit farther, the road meandered to an end with a sheep farm on both sides. A dog watched me as he stayed dry under a truck. Territorial Road was cut off here by I-94, and it looked like I had to turn around and detour.

However, as I reached the end of the road, I could see how Territorial Road resumes on the other side of the interstate. It was tantalizingly close. A detour was going to add three or four tough miles on a rainy day. I saw off to my left that the fence had been partly pushed down, and I impulsively decided to go for it. I disconnected the orange flag and tucked it under the seat of the Burley. I unfastened the Burley from my bike, and lifted the bike, then the Burley, and then myself over the fence. I had to struggle to push through heavy weeds and small trees to get to the edge of the highway. My spokes caught on the underbrush. Here I reattached the Burley. Now I had to get across this busy interstate. Waiting two or three full minutes before I saw a gap in traffic, I rushed across. Two huge semi-trucks, side-by-side, horns blaring, bore down on me. I gasped in relief as I reached the gap between the highway lanes. Unfortunately, there was also a crash fence in the median. I detached the Burley again, lifted everything over, and reattached. Then it was another long wait and a risky dash across the east-bound lanes. On the other side was still another fence, and even thicker woods. Persisting, I burst through on the other side.

In reality, I didn't cross the highway here. If I didn't have a wife and kids, if I wasn't worried about getting arrested, maybe even if it just hadn't been raining, I might have gone for it. I might have been able to follow the original course of the Territorial Road. Instead, feeling dejected and wimpy, I turned my bike around and went back down the gravel road.

And that's when I got a flat tire.

Of course it was raining. Of course it was the last day and I was tired. Of course I was worried about finishing on time. My orange flag drooped and sagged in the rain overlooking my deflated tire. It went through my head that perhaps after coming all this way, this could end my trip, short of my goal.

But then I remembered Dave.

I walked my bike about a quarter mile back to Dave's house. He had a garage to stay dry in, and had some tools and mechanical ability to help change the tire and fix the tube. We got it fixed, and I didn't have to call my wife and have her pick me up. Dave was just like those settlers back in the day, willing to help a stranded traveler. The rain drops dried on the orange flag.

I got over I-94 and back to Territorial Road, back to that stretch that had beckoned to me from the other side. It was a gravel road here, with an empty old brick house from the late 1800's. This stretch was once again much like the old road the pioneers traveled. I pedaled along the shore of a small lake. In the early days of the Territorial Road, this was known as Emerson's Prospect Lake. Emerson had a barn for travelers to shelter for the night. There was also a town planned and platted here, to be called Van Buren Centre, but like Sandstone back near Jackson, it was a dream dashed by the Panic of 1837, one of America's worst economic depressions.

Beyond this ghost town were some more gravel roads and I traveled through thick woods—perhaps the same woods the Mortons passed through in 1835. Just like in the old days, the woods here were interspersed with prairies—now modern prairies with corn already, on this June day, higher than knee-high.

The old road spilled out on a busy county road and back into the 21st century at a crossroads marked on the map as Fritzburg, the center of Hamilton Township. This township was named after Alexander Hamilton, a Founding Father who advocated a strong and active national government. Like those urban Democrats who lived uncomfortably near the founding spot of the Republican Party in Jackson, I doubt many of the farmers around Fritzburg are thanking Hamilton for his big national government views. Perhaps instead they would be thanking Aaron Burr for shooting him.

Fritzburg was another of those places that prospered from the Territorial Road, with Brown's Tavern stealing the stagecoach business from Keeler farther along the road. The area was also known in the late 1800's for "The Great Free Fair," organized by a local chapter of The Grange. The Grange was a national organization, a social outlet for frontier farmers who later got involved in politics, leading to the Populist

Party.   "The Great Free Fair" drew thousands of attendees and dozens of politicians.   "It began as a township fair, but soon claimed jurisdiction throughout the world," claimed one history of Van Buren County.

Besides the fair, Fritzburg had "a doctor, a blacksmith, a Baker, a Barber and two stock buyers." It has bubkas today.

Here the southward route of the road from Paw Paw turned once again west toward Lake Michigan. Part of this stretch of road was a tunnel of trees, trees big enough to have seen other travelers on the Territorial Road in the 1800's. The clearing skies in the west were still off on the horizon.

Eight miles down the road was Keeler, where the road took a jog south before resuming its westward path. "In the early days, the little village of Keelerville was a place of some importance," said a history of Van Buren County. Keeler lost the last of its importance just a few years ago, when the Keeler Keg and Kitchen, a popular music and drinking spot, burned down.

Across from the empty lot left from the Keeler Keg and Kitchen is the second-to-last commemorative boulder, "dedicated to the Pioneer Men and Women of Van Buren County, Memorial Day, May 30, 1916." The boulder and plaque were placed here by the "Keeler

Thursday Club," part of the Van Buren County Federation of Women's Clubs. The Federation was a Progressive Era group, where middle- and upper-class women came together to accomplish community-minded things like commemorative boulders. The Morton House, my ultimate goal, was originally started as a museum by the Federation of Women's Clubs, and they still ran it when I first got involved. I might very well have been the first and only male president of the Federation of Women's Clubs. My male ego was not too large to serve. I stopped here at the Keeler boulder for a picture and a snack.

Keeler's boulder, placed in 1916

As I was bicycling across Michigan, I had a sense and hope that we were in the third historic bicycle craze. The second craze was when I was growing up in the 1960's and 70's, and the first was way back in the 1890's. The main stimulus to the 1890's bicycle boom was the invention of a bike that ordinary people could ride. The previous model was that ridiculous-looking-big-front-wheel bicycle that I'd really like to try riding. The new "safety" bicycle had two matched wheels, a chain drive, and rubber tires. It was now more comfortable and convenient than a horse.

The Wright Brothers were a famous part of this bicycle craze at the end of the nineteenth century. Their bicycle shop is only a short distance from the old Territorial Road, moved now to the campus of Greenfield Village and the Henry Ford Museum in Dearborn. Orville and Wilbur were passionate bicyclists before they flew into history. Some say there was a connection between bikes and airplanes. It was said by bicyclists in the late 1800's that "Wheeling is just like flying." And in some sense, one turns a bike by leaning, not steering, the same way an airplane leans into a turn.

This bicycle craze also changed history for women. The "New Woman" of the turn of the century rode bicycles just like the men. It led to dress reform for

137

women, as bustles and hoop skirts were major impediments to biking. The bicycle also enabled women to escape the prying eyes of chaperones. Bicycling had "done more to emancipate women than anything else in the world," said Susan B. Anthony. Fellow suffragette Frances Willard, who learned to ride a bike at age 53, told of women "acquiring this new implement of power and literally putting it underfoot."

Between Keeler and Millburg, I started to see orchards of peach, apple, and cherry trees. The "lake effect" makes this part of the state "Michigan's Fruitbelt." Eleazar Morton and his son Henry, in 1840, planted a ten-acre orchard of apple, peach, pear, plum and apricot trees.

The rain lightened and finally stopped as I entered Millburg. The sun brightened the orange of my Burley flag. I was reminded of the old days of the Territorial Road as I went by the Millburg Trading Post, White Horse Farms, and Chief's Bar.

Here my son Drew met me and unloaded his bike from the family van to ride the last seven miles into Benton Harbor. We stopped for a few minutes at the Blue Dress Barn, now a fashionable, if rustic, place for weddings. In the old days, it was a dairy barn for the House of David.

The House of David was a religious commune in Benton Harbor, known for being vegetarians, celibate, running a popular amusement park, and having nationally-known baseball teams. The men also had waist-length hair. The charismatic leaders of the community were Benjamin Purnell (known to outsiders as King Ben), and his wife Mary Purnell. Of course, a sex scandal was part of the local legend.

Drew and I also made a short stop at a church youth group car wash fundraiser. I donated $5 and got a bike baptism and chocolate chip cookies in return! I now was able to ride a clean and shiny bike on the last stretch of my journey. I was shedding the old dirt from my spokes and my life.

As I rode into the small city of Benton Harbor, I was in some sense coming home. I lived here, on Territorial Road, in a handsome Victorian house with a wonderful wrap-around porch, for nine years. Outwardly, I did not fit into Benton Harbor. I was a white, suburban, middle-class guy, while Benton Harbor is 92% African-American, mostly poor. But this fascinating city fit me in many ways.

I had lived in similar areas in Washington, D.C. during a three- year dalliance with a career in government. When I moved back home to the area to teach high school, I was searching for both a church and good projects to involve my students in history. I found both on Morton Hill in Benton Harbor. I don't remember which was first. First Presbyterian Church provided independence from the church I grew up in, while being theologically familiar. The Morton Cemetery was an overgrown patch of history, waiting for students to sweat and learn. Both places sucked me into the life of Benton Harbor.

I later fell in love with the Sowers House, built circa 1903. And I got drafted into a wonderful circle of volunteers at the Morton House, although once again, I did not fit into this group of ladies who were often focused on 19th century dishes and linens and dresses.

As a Chicago Cubs fan, I've always been on the side of the underdog. Benton Harbor has been in that category from the start. Stanley Morton, the grandson of Eleazar, told the story of the birth of the city in the late 1850's. The bridge from Benton Harbor to St. Joseph was wiped out in a flood, and some of the leading residents of Benton Harbor went up the hill to plead with St. Joseph to help rebuild the bridge connecting the two cities. The story goes that the St. Joseph fathers looked down the hill and down their noses at the Benton Harbor folks, and refused them flat.

This spurred the Benton Harbor citizens to build a canal instead, which led to the founding of Benton Harbor.

Benton Harbor was also an underdog when I moved there. The city was a classic example of the death of inner cities in America. Benton Harbor saw white flight and racism, suburbanization and the interstate highways, the loss of American and Rust Belt manufacturing. These factors resulted in Benton Harbor going from a leading prosperous city to a down-on-its-luck ghetto. I swear I once saw sagebrush rolling along Main Street as I came home from college in 1981.

But Benton Harbor was starting a comeback in the early 1990's, and it seemed exciting to be a part of it. I was often dubbed a "pioneer" in my urban "frontier" neighborhood. I knew what they meant, although I was no more a pioneer in this already-settled neighborhood than the western settlers heading into an American west already populated by Native Americans.

Creativity led the way to revitalizing Benton Harbor. A few visionaries set up arts-related businesses in deserted downtown buildings. Critical mass was achieved, and today Benton Harbor's downtown is a place to create, hang out, and eat. The Morton House also experienced a renaissance, going from a dusty house museum to a more dynamic "Home of Benton

Harbor History." Our aim was to be part of the revitalization of the city. My bike ride down Territorial Road was part of that mission and part of coming home to Benton Harbor.

Our rate of pedaling increased as we got close to the end. We passed the Morton Cemetery, where the Morton family and Jackson Prison warden Alonzo Vincent are buried. Large pines and maples watch over the 19th and early 20th century tombstones here.

As a teacher, I used to bring students here to do history projects. In 1989, we had a group of kids in the cemetery cutting the grass, planting flowers, and doing chalk rubbings of tombstones. Early in the day, a student came up to me and said, "Mr. Jager, look what I found." In his hand was the top of a human skull. A bit later, the students found the rest of the skeleton. This has to top the list of field trip nightmares for a teacher. It turned out to be an 1800's accidental exhumation, not a murder victim, and I had a great story to tell future students when we visited the cemetery.

I was nearing the end of my trip. Across the state, I had been searching for signs of the original travelers of this road back in the 1830's. Although traces of humans from the 19th century were scarce, one visible witness to that past still remained—trees. At various points on my trip down the road, I had passed large oaks or maples that certainly had also been seen by the early pioneers like the Mortons.

Here in the Morton Hill neighborhood in Benton Harbor were two remarkable trees that were already mature when the Mortons first came. Just kitty-corner from my old house was an enormous cottonwood tree, with a small stone marker at its base that indicated the tree was used as a boundary marker in the early days of Benton Harbor's settlement. When I lived there, this tree always gave a nice reminder of winter in June, when it showered down a blizzard of white fluffy seeds.

The other notable tree was just across from the Morton House Museum. This was an oak tree that was estimated to be up to 400 years old. It towers on top of the hill overlooking downtown Benton Harbor. The Morton oak even has its own lot and bank account. The previous owners next door to the tree deeded the lot to the Morton House Museum to protect it from removal and development. A fund was established for maintenance, and one of my jobs at the Morton House Museum is to mow the lawn under its spreading branches.

The next few blocks past the cemetery were, in the early 1900's, a grand street. Doctors, lawyers, and other professionals built large Victorian homes.

Just two blocks before Drew and I reached the Morton House, my final destination, I passed my old house, the Sowers House. Bouton Sowers was a medical doctor and a member of the Benton Harbor school board. The house was a solid and unpretentious Victorian—not a "painted lady!" It featured five bedrooms, a steeply-sloping roof, and wide brick fireplace. The main attraction was the porch, which wrapped from the front around the side, enclosing a beautiful corner bay with six tall windows. A former resident of the neighborhood told me of walking past this house and often seeing Mrs. Sowers sitting in the bay, doing her sewing.

I was also drawn to what was not on the house. A 1915 business-boosting book showcased the Sowers' house. In this century-old photo, the bay featured a railing on top of the second floor, crowning the house. When I moved in, it was gone. It called to me to be replaced, and I built a suitable replica and had it attached.

I also loved the house's diamond pane windows. But this love came with labor. The house had fifty of these windows, and they all needed to be reglazed. I was dating my future wife, Mary Jo, at this time. She certainly showed her love by helping to reglaze all 50 windows, most with small diamond panes. We later added a white picket fence, built an arbor gate, and completely rebuilt the rotted roof of the detached carriage house featuring barn doors. We evicted the carpenter ants from the rotting wood on the side of the house. We repainted, replacing the dirty mustard yellow with a stately gray, complimented by dark gray and burgundy accents.

The house across the side street from mine, also on Territorial, was equally fascinating. This house was the Ryno House, but also known as "The Mayors' House," lived in by two early mayors of Benton Harbor. When I moved into the neighborhood, it was empty and almost overrun by ivy. We watched the house's renovation out our bedroom windows. Sadly, it was never quite completed. It was, and is, a striking house. It is one of those houses you just keeping looking at, finding new and interesting features. The Ryno house has a covered front porch with an open balcony above it. An open half-circle bay is on one side, while the other side has a lower door surrounded by a field stone arch and side pillars. Above this is a jutting bay window, with a seat inside that beckons you to read a book in the morning sunshine. The third floor has pebble stone attic accents. There is dentilation, carved wreaths...oh, maybe you should just buy it and live there.

The last house on Territorial Road was my destination, the Morton House. It is the oldest house in Benton Harbor and home to three generations of local history makers. Eleazar Morton came from New York state and traveled the Territorial Road 179 years before I did. He stopped briefly in Galesburg (had those cronuts been around back then he might have stayed) and came to Benton Harbor in 1836. While his home was not officially a tavern, many travelers on the Territorial Road spent a night at the Morton homestead before crossing the river to the St. Joseph harbor. Victor Gore, a prominent Benton Harbor lawyer, told of this early "tavern:"

"On the high ground on the present Main Street, in front of the Premier Hotel, he built a log house, choosing this site, probably, because of a spring of excellent water which he found there. At that time the farmers, from as far east as Kalamazoo, brought their produce to the St. Joseph harbor and after the building of the Morton home, they found it convenient to time their journey so that they might reach the Morton's at dark, spend the night there, go to St. Joseph, by way of the old Spink's bridge and back—a trip, which in those days, took a day—spend another night at the Morton's and get an early start for home the next morning. The Morton home was none too large for the Morton family, so in order to make his uninvited guests comfortable, Eleazar Morton was practically obliged, at the end of the first year, to raise the loft into sleeping quarters, build an addition to his house and again become a tavern keeper."

In 1849, Eleazar and his son Henry built a plain farmhouse on what became known as Morton Hill. (Favorite quote from Eleazar—"Henry lived with me until I lived with Henry.) A local newspaper account described their neighborhood in the early 1800s and also gave some insight into racial attitudes back in the day: "Huge timber then covered the now cultivated and built up Morton Hill and the redskins roamed the forest while the busy white man led a strenuous existence."

Eleazar was certainly a patriot. When he fell deathly ill in January, 1864, he predicted to his family that he would live to see Independence Day. He died July 4, 1864. His son Henry was one of the founders of the city of Benton Harbor in 1866, and his grandson James Stanley Morton was head of the Graham and Morton steamship line, which brought fruit to Chicago and tourists to Benton Harbor and St. Joseph. The line promoted itself with two great tag lines: "The Dustless Road to Happyland," and "The Steel Fleet of White Flyers."

Stanley renovated the Morton House in 1912, creating the elegant 19th century home that now houses a museum. He added upscale upgrades like the large columns on the front porch, birds'-eye maple trim, and a Pullman Railroad window.

At 2:15 p.m. on Saturday, Drew and I pulled into the Morton House, past the last commemorative boulder, with my mother, my wife and other son Sam, and members of the Morton House Board there to greet us. I stored my Burley in the family van, and laid the orange flag there for a final rest.

The end of the Territorial Road, Benton Harbor

This last boulder marking the Territorial Road was dedicated almost exactly 100 years before my trip. The DAR was once again the driving force, in this case the local Algonquin chapter. At that 1915 dedication, the opening prayer was by the minister of the First Presbyterian Church, located right on Territorial a block away. Nathan Lovell, an early pioneer as a boy, shared his memories of early life along the road. In his remarks, he called the Territorial Road "the grandest road in Michigan."

Two young "lads" then unveiled the boulder and tablet, and the head of the DAR presented the monument to the city. She noted that J. Stanley Morton had procured the boulder from a farm in Millburg, east of this spot on the Territorial Road. The mayor gave a speech, the DAR members recited the Pledge of Allegiance, and some schoolchildren "joyously rendered" the song "America."

This marker, like the ones in Ann Arbor and Galesburg, had some trouble along the way. At some point, the brass plaque was pried off the boulder. Fortunately, the plaque was recovered and hung inside the Morton House Museum, while the boulder was engraved with information from the plaque.

This was the symbolic end of the road, but I had more to do to complete the trip. The Territorial Road continues for a bit in Benton Harbor, ending in the vibrant Arts District that has jumpstarted the renaissance of Benton Harbor. I coasted down Morton Hill into downtown Benton Harbor, Burleyless, triumphant and relieved.

As I rode this last stretch of Territorial Road, I could imagine the ghosts of yesteryear in this once and future thriving city. To my right, just below Morton Hill, I could imagine the small houses, groceries and smells of

Little Italy. I crossed Ox Creek, perhaps named after the many oxen that pulled wagons across Michigan and over this last, narrow obstacle. Looking down Sixth Street to my left, I could see the ghosts of hundreds of wagons loaded with apples, pears, peaches, or cherries, part of the huge open air fruit market that gathered on this street each day in the summer and fall. To my right down Fifth Street, would have wafted the sulfurous smells of the old mineral baths of the Saltzmann and Dwan Hotels. I could almost hear the clanking and neighing from the old Livery, now a popular entertainment and craft beer spot. On the north side of Territorial stands the old Federal Building, awaiting new condos, but I could imagine the hustle and bustle of the old Post Office.

I reached the end of Territorial Road in Benton Harbor, where it intersects Water Street. Here I could imagine more spots that were now just ghosts—the lively Nick's Bar in the Michigan Hotel on my left; gas station attendants checking the oil on the right; the charred ruins of the tragic Yore Opera House just behind me. The beautiful architecture of the 1890's Hinckley Building, brings back ghosts of the Victorian era. Peeking around the corner of the Hinckley Building, I can almost hear the boat whistles of the White Flyers of the

Graham and Morton steamship line as they unload tourists from Chicago in the turning basin at the end of the ship canal. Looking behind me, I can almost see Stanley Morton putt-putting his way down Territorial to his office overlooking the turning basin.

This spot was once the heart of a thriving city. During the 1980's, though, Territorial was the road that my wife and I walked our dogs and nodded hello to the ladies of the evening. We pushed our kids' strollers past garbage and abandoned houses. Today it is the lively nucleus of the Arts District. Standing on the corner of Territorial and Water, I could see galleries, hip restaurants, and bars, a music venue and craft beer spot in the old Livery. I could smell the barbecue. I could see the flowers of well-tended parks, and ride new bike lanes. Territorial Road here brings new pioneers to Benton Harbor.

Then I continued on into the sister city of St. Joseph, where there is another plaque marking the Territorial Road on the side of an old bank. St. Joseph has a much earlier history than the rest of the towns along the Territorial Road, except for Detroit. It was originally the site of Fort Miami, established by the French voyageurs in the 1600's.

This is also the site of the landing of the famous French explorer LaSalle, who was waiting for his resupply ship *Griffon*. When it never showed—the wreck has never been found—LaSalle set out on foot for Detroit and Canada. It is likely he went down the Indian footpath that eventually became the Territorial Road, in the opposite direction of my journey.

I rode down to Silver Beach in St. Joseph. My bike computer showed 200.12 miles. Total riding time was 16 hours and 56 minutes, with an average speed of 11.81 miles per hour. I rode down to the water and stuck my front wheel in Lake Michigan. My journey was complete.

But it wasn't complete. A gap in my map called to me. One section of the road remained untraced. And this section would bring me closer to the pioneers than any other part of the Territorial Road.

The gap was the six miles that ran through the Fort Custer Training Center, just west of Battle Creek. Fort Custer was a military base and home to 12 units of the Army Reserve and National Guard. When I researched the road and saw it ran through the base, my heart sank. After 9/11 and other terrorist attacks, I thought the chances were slim that the military would let a civilian ride his bike through the base.

I was wrong. I contacted Master Sargent John Marietta, the military liaison to the post's museum. With one understandable exception, Marietta could not have been more helpful to my trip. He gave permission over the phone, and asked when I was coming through. I told him, and he said, "No way. Any day except that one." Murphy's Law--the base was hosting a major training exercise that day. So I went back the week after my trip to ride the last uncompleted miles.

I met Master Sargent Marietta at his office, and I put my bike in the back of his pickup. He drove me to the easternmost spot of the Territorial Road on the base, and wished me good luck. I could see the Battle Creek airport on the other side of the fence. I started down the road.

And I went back to the 1830's.

I was now on a lonely two-track, surrounded by uninhabited woods. I traveled past wetlands with only frogs, snakes, and swans. Occasionally the woods opened to prairies and farm fields of settlers who had preceded me down the road. As I cleared a rise, I surprised a coyote with a rabbit in his mouth. After a couple of miles, I came across an old, seldom-visited cemetery.   I imagined the disappointment of the pioneers as I saw:

Julie Ann Burdick
Died August 22, 1847
Aged 1 year and 14 days

The old map showed a school and houses near here, but if the foundations remained, the woods were hiding them.

But the woods also hid modern civilization. This stretch of the Territorial Road, preserved by a military base, brought me closest to the traveling experience of the Michigan pioneers of the 1830's. I couldn't hear the traffic on I-94. I knew it was only three or four miles from this spot. But for this moment, at this spot, the modern Interstate and the pioneer Territorial Road were almost two centuries apart.

My journey along the Territorial Road was at an end. So was my search—for history along a road, for a welcoming bicycling environment, and for a new beginning for me as an author

This trip started my new journey as a writer. As I rode the road and wrote this book, I often thought of

Eleazar Morton guiding a wagon through the wilderness on the Territorial Road. Writing the story of my trip, page by page, connected me to Eleazar and his son Henry as they built their new home in Benton Harbor, brick by brick.

If I was looking for bicycle bliss, I did not find it on the Territorial Road. Instead, the road is testament that the car is king, especially in Michigan. Only rarely did I find some kind of space or consideration for the cyclist. Mostly, the route is designed for cars, and stressful and dangerous for bicycles. I found history, but I did not see a good future for cyclists on Territorial Road.

While it was not an easy bicycle trip, my spot on top of a bicycle showed me plenty of historical sites. Michigan's Territorial Road is truly a historical road in that a number of important events occurred near its path. Many were of local and state importance, like Tiger Stadium, the Morton Homestead, the many mansions of Marshall, and the historic taverns along the way. But I was pleased to find history of national import. Along this key Michigan roadway the Republican Party was born. Sojourner Truth certainly often traveled this path as she lived and died in Battle Creek. Near the Territorial Road in Dearborn, the traveler can discover the history of both Rosa Parks and

Mayor Hubbard. And while Territorial Road was originally an Indian path, it opened the state to intruders that completely altered the lives of tribes like the Potawatomi.

I found history, but only rarely did I find the pioneer path across a wilderness. Much of my journey would be unrecognizable and perhaps incomprehensible to the Morton family of 1835.

Certainly the historical road was hard to find on the eastern side of the state: the towering buildings and crowded streets of downtown Detroit, the empty storefronts of western Detroit, and the urban sprawl between Dearborn and Ann Arbor.

But as I traveled westward, glimpses of the old road were there. It took some imagination, but I could see the Mortons' wagons rolling past the historic taverns of Marshall, and cresting the hill near Battle Creek that opened on the Gogouac Prairie.

More clearly, I could imagine the Mortons and other pioneers on the two-track in the woods and marshes of Ft. Custer. I felt just a bit of the frustration of the pioneers with a breakdown along the road in the wildness west of Paw Paw. I was with the Mortons on the dirt roads in Van Buren County, past the pockets of prairie amidst the deep dark woods. Finally, my homecoming at the end of the trip was the home of the Mortons, and the home of Benton Harbor history.

I was more than two centuries away from the Mortons' trip, but my journey took me down their path. I now looked forward to the new journey I started by following Eleazar. My bicycle tires rolled in the ruts of their historic wagons.

Back in time
The Territorial Road through Ft.Custer

Acknowledgments

A heartfelt thank you to those people who helped the long-time dream to write a book come true: Christy Sloan, who encouraged me to include myself in this book; Rich Pender, who offered the gifts of writerly craftsmanship and camaraderie; and Denise Tackett, who provided important finishing touches. Any mistakes remaining in the book were found by them, but left in the manuscript because of my stubbornness and silly sense of style.

Thank you also to those who provided pioneer hospitality along the road: Lori Ward and Scott Munzel; Pa Smith; Craig "Doc" Warner.

Many thanks also to those history folks who provided valuable information and guidance, including Karen Wisniewski and Karen Krepps at the Dearborn Historical Society; James Mann in Ypsilanti, Jan Tobin at the Washtenaw County Historical Society, Susan Van Zandt at the Honolulu House in Marshall, John Marietta of Fort Custer Training Center, and especially Kay Maxon, the heart of Galesburg.

Thanks also to Mari Maloney with help with the pixels.

Lastly, thank you to Janet Frazier, whose hand-drawn maps were the perfect addition to the book.

64690261R00101

Made in the USA
Lexington, KY
16 June 2017